Reading Difficulties in Schools

A Community Study of Specific Reading Difficulties,
Carried Out with a Grant from the
Scottish Education Department

Margaret M. Clark

Penguin Books

Penguin Books Ltd, Harmondsworth,
Middlesex, England
Penguin Books Inc., 7110 Ambassador Road,
Baltimore, Md 21207, U.S.A.
Penguin Books Australia Ltd,
Ringwood, Victoria, Australia

First published 1970
Copyright © Margaret M. Clark, 1970

Made and printed in Great Britain by
C. Nicholls & Company Ltd
Set in Monotype Times New Roman

Penguin Education

Penguin Papers in Education

Reading Difficulties in Schools

Margaret M. Clark

To Robert R. Rusk

Publisher's Note

'Research results that remain on the shelf,' the Secretary of State for Education has recently said, 'are a waste of public money. We must all pay far more attention to dissemination.'

Penguin Papers in Education is an attempt to close the gap between research and action. The series will present important work on all levels of education in a form that will make real sense to teachers, educationalists and students.

The publishers will be pleased to hear from research workers and departments who are concerned to communicate their findings to a wide audience.

Contents

Part Four
Summary and Implications

List of Tables and Figures

Appendix

Figures

Preface

The earliest reports of children of average intelligence who yet appeared to have severe difficulty with reading were made in 1896. There has been an upsurge of interest in this aspect of reading difficulty, which has been variously described as *word blindness*, *dyslexia*, or *specific reading disability*. Case-records of such children have been compared with groups of 'normal' children; symposia with contributions from specialists on the disabilities of these children have been presented; the press and and television have highlighted the problems of such children. Teachers and parents have been made aware of the existence of such cases and are being warned to pay attention to the needs of these children. Books on dyslexia are mainly by neurologists, while references in the work of psychologists have tended to be less wholeheartedly in support of the view that dyslexia is a useful concept. Some writers have confined their use of the word 'dyslexia' to children of average intelligence who, in the absence of poor vision, defective hearing or high absence-rate, and in spite of remedial tuition, are still severely backward in reading. Others have used a wider definition and included children of average intelligence who have not made the progress in reading expected on the basis of their intelligence; or children who have spelling or writing difficulties. For some, dyslexia is the term describing all backward readers.

A great deal of misunderstanding has arisen from all these differences in usage, which have not always been clearly specified. A difference in labelling has tended to arise, depending on whether the child happens to be referred to a psychologist or a neurologist – the latter often using dyslexia as a diagnostic label, the former rarely. Unfortunately there have been a number of clashes between protagonists with different points of view, none of which has helped to clarify the position for those outside the immediate centre of controversy. In a recent article in

Educational Research called 'Dyslexia – a problem of communication', Jessie Reid (1968) discusses the difficulties with examples of statements by various contributors to the controversy.

It was felt by the present writer that some light might be thrown on this whole area by a study which began with a complete community study, in order to ascertain the extent to which certain variables suggested as being significant in dyslexia are related to early reading progress in children – ability to differentiate right and left, motor co-ordination, left-handedness, etc. Teachers may well interpret statements of factors associated with severe reading difficulty as of relevance to them in their everyday teaching experiences. It is therefore important to study these within a normal population, and this was the aim of the first part of this present study. A group of 1544 children was used for this part of the research, which forms Part One of the book. The next stage involved 230 of these children who were having difficulty with reading after 2 years at school. This group was studied further at 8 years of age, and an analysis made of their level of intelligence. Spelling errors were also studied to determine whether reversals of letters or letter-order are a common or rare occurrence in children who have difficulty with reading. Here again it is important to the attitude of both parents and teachers that they know how commonly these characteristics are to be expected in a child who is a backward reader. This study of *all* the backward readers forms Part Two. Finally, a further analysis was made of those who were found to be of average intelligence and continued to have difficulty with reading, to determine both the size of this problem and the other features which were associated with it. This aspect is discussed in Part Three.

No selection has taken place during the study except on the basis of the criterion of either reading or intelligence, and presence in a school in the county in which the study has been conducted. The importance of this characteristic of the present research lies in the fact that these are *not* clinic cases, but *all* such cases of that age in the county. Children with reading difficulty are referred to a clinic not solely on the basis of that problem. The presence of such facilities, and awareness of them by teachers and parents; sensitivity of parents to their children's difficulties; and the extent to which the child's level deviates from the family level – all will influence *whether* a child is referred. Reading level need not determine *where* he is referred – he could be seen by the county psychologist, by his family doctor or a neurologist, by a speech therapist or in a private clinic for reading difficulties. Thus the type of facilities available, the size of waiting lists, and views of the parents may all influence whether, and where, a child with reading difficulties is sent for assistance. If one is to make a realistic assessment of the prevalence of, and need for provision for, a certain disability, the community is the appropriate source of information rather than incidence figures from clinics. Nevertheless, it is of course essential to assess the extent to which the results are influenced by the particular community selected.

The method of presentation of the results of this study has been planned to enable its findings to be appreciated by as wide a public as possible. It is hoped, however, that the results will *not* be used as further fuel for the controversy, but as the basis for a more realistic assessment of the community needs of children with continuing difficulty in reading and spelling. The extent and the severity of this problem should not be under-estimated, but let us not fall into the trap of thinking that a diagnostic label and a single remedial method employed by a teacher who is trained to apply that method, but who has little knowledge of the wider areas of reading problems, is the answer. It is an attractive simple solution, but not one in keeping with the findings of the present research.

Over eighty people have assisted directly either with the testing or the analysis of data for this project over the past three years; it is therefore not possible to mention them all by name. I hope that all those who are not acknowledged in this way will accept my grateful thanks and will believe that their help was no less appreciated.

I am grateful to the Scottish Education Department which, by a grant of £4500 over a two-year period, has made the research possible; and to the University of Strathclyde which, by permitting me to undertake the research, has carried the hidden financial costs. I would like to express my particular thanks to Mr J. G. Morris of the Scottish Education Department, who has assisted the research at every stage and in every way since its inception. I am grateful to Mr A. B. Cameron, Director of Education for Dunbartonshire, and his staff for permitting me to carry out the study in the county, and to Mr J. Murray Allan for smoothing my path throughout. My thanks also to the head teachers and their staffs who bore with such good-natured tolerance our letters, visits and inquiries. Thanks to them, the only children who escaped were those who moved to 'foreign parts'.

It was originally planned to have a full-time research assistant on the project, but only during the early stages was this possible for any length of time, when Mr L. Leigh Lucas assisted with the project. I would like to express my gratitude particularly to Mrs Anna Greenwood, Miss Jennifer Russell and Mrs Christina Del Priore, all of whom worked nearly full-time in a part-time capacity. Volunteer students and staff from Notre Dame College of Education, students from Jordanhill College of Education and from Strathclyde University all assisted with the early testing. I would like to mention especially Miss Margaret Paul, who, from being a volunteer student in the early days, went on to assist at progressively more advanced levels; another Strathclyde student, Mr Cameron Cunningham, who assisted in the preparation of the manuscript for publication; and Mrs E. Elder, who painstakingly typed my many drafts.

My thanks are also due to Dr W. Wilson of the Royal Infirmary, Glasgow, for allowing Dr Martin on his staff to carry out the vision testing, to the County School Health Service for making the arrangements, and to the Western Regional Hospital Board for allowing Mrs Beattie and Miss Auld to perform the audiometric testing. I am grateful to Mr W. Yule and Dr M. Rutter of the Institute of Psychiatry, London University, who have been so willing to share information from the Isle of Wight Survey; and to Dr T. Ingram of the Department of Child Life and Health, Edinburgh University, for allowing me to use a modified version of the articulation test he is developing.

Dr A. Pilliner of the Godfrey Thomson Unit for Educational Research is acting as statistical consultant to the project. This was not arranged until the testing was complete, so he cannot be held responsible for any deficiencies in the planning of the project. I am extremely grateful both to Dr Pilliner and to Mr Michael Hutchings of the same department for their assistance in the analysis of the enormous amount of data which has been assembled. With their help further and more sophisticated analyses are being performed. The computing facilities at the University of Strathclyde have been used, and programmes written by Mr Clive Payne and Mr W. Miller.

It seemed important to communicate the preliminary results of the research to as wide a public as possible and as quickly as possible. For the opportunity to do this, I am grateful to the staff of Penguin Education.

In dedicating this work to Dr Robert R. Rusk, whose teaching so strongly influenced not only my interest in, but also my approach to educational research, I would like to pay tribute to the part he has played in the development of a tradition of educational research in Scotland which makes a research worker so readily accepted in a Scottish school.

Chapter 1
Introduction: Backwardness in Reading

There are children who learn to read with little or no formal instruction; at the other extreme are those for whom learning to read is a slow, laborious process. For the majority, however, learning to read is more or less enjoyable and more or less successful depending on the school environment in which the learning takes place. A group of children all of the same age, and the same length of time at school, will show marked differences in reading ability. The better the teaching, the higher the level of the class; yet a range of differences will still remain.

The Home

Many of the factors which influence *relative* progress in learning to read are to a great extent outside the control of the teacher. Some children start school with an adequate vocabulary, both spoken and understood, with wide experience, both general and of books, all of which make them ready and eager to start learning to read. For these children, once they start school, the home reinforces the school learning situation. At the other extreme is the child who comes to school almost inarticulate, never having learnt to listen, having had few experiences, or few that will facilitate the task of the teacher. In some such instances, however, once such a child comes to school the parents, if not widening the child's learning experiences, do at least appreciate and support the teacher in her role. Unfortunately, all too often in the case of the child who needs it most, the support is not forthcoming.

Changes of school, even within a single administrative area, may result in quite different approaches to the teaching of reading; the less stable the staffing in individual schools, the more difficult it is to take sufficiently into account the needs of the child with frequent changes of school. Absence, while partly conditioned by ill-health, is also influenced by home environment and the attitude of the parents to school. Total absence does not give the whole picture; at least as difficult to allow for is a pattern of irregular attendance.

The School

Many of the researches into factors leading to backwardness in school work have stressed the importance of the home environment, following the classical studies of Sir Cyril Burt (1961), first published in 1937, who revealed the striking difference in incidence of backwardness in different areas of London. In her recent study in Kent Dr Joyce Morris (1966) has stressed the fact that in many cases school circumstances may reinforce the difficulties of the children most handicapped by home circumstances. The role of the teachers has also been highlighted in that study: both the role of the head teacher as the co-ordinator of the school policy with regard to reading, and the members of staff who, by their enthusiasm and skill, will be major contributing factors to the standard of reading achieved in their school.

Investigations into the effect of different teaching methods on level of reading skills have all come to the same conclusion: that though in the short term a new method may appear to improve the standards of reading, in the long-term analysis there is *no single best method of teaching reading* (Chall, 1967; Burt, 1969). Some methods are better for some children; some methods are better used by some teachers. The teacher is the important variable. What is important is that the teacher, whatever method she uses, is aware of the individual members of her class and prepared to vary the approach to take account of their strengths and weaknesses.

The Child

General intellectual ability will affect the speed at which a child grasps a new process, the amount of repetition required to learn new material, and the complexity of the tasks he can accomplish at a given age. Such factors will influence to some extent the child's progress in learning the basic mechanics of reading, and will have even greater effect as silent reading for comprehension becomes the main reading task. Specific abilities will also play their part in determining progress. A good visual memory, particularly important for word recognition, will enable a child, after little repetition, to gain an adequate sight vocabulary preparatory to his first steps in reading, while the child with a good auditory memory, combined with good auditory discrimination, will quickly master the intricacies of phonic analysis.

Factors such as adequate hearing and vision will both play a part in determining a child's progress. Here one has to distinguish those abilities which are *essential* in learning to read from those whose importance is magnified by the group situation in which most children are taught to read – a very large group in many instances. Total or severe deafness would be a serious handicap in learning to read; on the other hand, partial deafness could have severe effect on a child's progress in the class-group situation, particularly when the extraneous noise-level is high – a hazard which many teachers and children have to tolerate. It is the same with vision; a greater visual acuity is required to distinguish visual aids in a classroom than would be required for the reading task itself.

Ability to concentrate is important to success in the early stages of learning to read, where the child has to stay with the task long enough to acquire an adequate sight vocabulary before he will get the satisfaction of getting meaning from the printed page. Here the skill of the teacher, her ability to vary the presentation so that frequent repetition is achieved without boredom, with material geared to the children's interests, will influence the way her class copes with the situation. It is important, however, to consider the extent to which general immaturity causes a child to fail in the learning situation, and the extent to which the failure is the result of the circumstances which place him in a group-learning situation at a time which is inopportune *for him*. Unfortunately in the British school system, as in others, there are some learning situations which are presented when the majority are ready for them, and should a particular child not be ready *at that time* his opportunity has passed.

Influences on progress in reading – some outside the control of the teacher, others which she has to accept – act differentially on the children in her class, and mean that the rate of progress to be expected will vary from school to school, and within a class from child to child. Researches indicate that, just as there is no single best method of teaching reading, cases of severe backwardness in reading *seldom result from a single cause*, but usually from several adverse influences acting together on the child (Burt, 1961; Robinson, 1946; Malmquist, 1958).

Specific Reading Disability

Specific reading disability, *dyslexia* or *word blindness* are terms used to describe children who fail to learn to read in spite of normal intelligence, intact senses, proper instruction and normal motivation. In an article in the *Lancet* in 1895 James Hinshelwood, a Glasgow eye specialist, discussed word blindness and visual memory. About the same time a general practitioner, Dr Pringle Morgan, and a medical officer, James Kerr, each reported a case of an intelligent boy who had failed to learn to read.* Since then a controversy has raged, with conflicting opinions being offered regarding the importance of this disability as a cause of a failure to learn to read. There are instances of adults who through known brain injury have lost the power either to read or write, while even possibly retaining the ability to recognize individual letters. Description of such cases is found in the neurological literature, but such cases are mercifully rare. There are also instances of children suffering from identified brain injury with resulting impairment of specific functions, though in young children the results of brain injury may sometimes be transitory, as other areas of the brain may take over the functions of the damaged area in a way that would not happen in an adult, where the functions of the brain are more localized. The controversy is *not* about such cases of identified gross brain damage, but the extension of this concept to a *developmental* one, where a child has failed to acquire the ability to read and spell, or achieved limited success *in the absence of gross neurological impairment*. Patients referred to neurologists, not because of a

* See Critchley (1964) and Malmquist (1958) for a discussion of the early studies of word blindness.

medical disorder, but because of a failure to learn to read, have been investigated in an attempt to discover precisely what other symptoms these cases have in common.

Dyslexia, a term used synonomously with *word blindness* for cases of severe reading difficulty, is claimed by some clinicians to be found only in patients of average or superior intelligence, though others would not confine the concept of dyslexia to those of average intelligence, but would argue that it is a disability that can affect children of any level of intelligence. It is also claimed that cases of dyslexia use bizarre spelling, with confusions of letters, reversals of letters and words; that frequently they have a poor memory for sounds in sequence and/or poor motor co-ordination; slow speech development; left-handedness; crossed-laterality (with preferred hand and eye different); doubtful dominance (or a family history of these); and often a history of reading difficulty in the family (see Hallgren, 1950). Many factors have been mentioned as characteristic of such cases, or found in the majority of cases, but none has been found in all such cases. In Britain clinicians such as Dr Macdonald Critchley in London, Professor Zangwill in Cambridge and Dr Ingram in Edinburgh are working in this field. In Copenhagen a Word Blind Centre was established in 1939, and in 1963 one was opened in London. In the United States there are many clinics specializing in such cases. There is still no real agreement on diagnostic criteria, however, nor on the approximate incidence of the disorder in the child population, whether it is a rare phenomenon or a major consideration for those involved in teaching children to read. What is the magnitude of the 'at risk' population, and how can it be identified? This is a question of some practical concern to educators, but no clear-cut answer is to be found in the available literature.* The incidence has been put at anything from 1 to 10 per cent (or even 20 per cent), with boys at greater risk than girls; while some psychologists, on the basis of large-scale surveys,

* No attempt has been made in the list of references to give an exhaustive bibliography of the literature on dyslexia. Attention is drawn however to the work of the following: Critchley (1964), Crosby and Liston (1968), Doehring (1968), and the two symposia edited by Money, and Money and Schiffman (1962 and 1966).

have felt that this concept adds little to our understanding of reading backwardness (Morris, 1966; Daniels, in Franklin, 1958; Malmquist, 1958).

The aim of the research analysed in this book was to investigate the incidence of severe reading disability in a normal school population – that is, cases of children who have severe difficulty in learning to read which cannot be explained adequately in other terms. The study was so planned that incidence figures in the community for the various characteristics associated with dyslexia could be determined – based on the population from which the cases of severe reading disability were drawn – something which is not usually possible in clinical studies of a disorder. It was hoped that such an investigation would:

1. Give *incidence* figures for severe reading disability in the population, thereby indicating *the size of the provision* required to cater for the problem.

2. Indicate the *pattern* of the disabilities associated with severe reading disability, thereby suggesting the *type of provision* required.

3. Suggest ways of *identifying* such children as soon as possible, in an attempt *to prevent* severe reading disability from developing.

The term 'dyslexia' has been applied in many ways, including to all children who have severe difficulty in reading; or only those of a given level of intelligence who have severe difficulty; or those who have not made the progress predicted on the basis of their intelligence; or even children with writing and spelling difficulties possibly associated with difficulty in reading. For this reason the term is not used in this study, in which the broadest terms of reference have been taken in an attempt to analyse the types of disability found within a single community, uncommitted to any particular diagnostic label. This study was neither planned to prove the existence nor the absence of dyslexia; the terms used within each phase of the study are therefore meant only to be descriptive of the criteria of selection. The three phases are as follows:

1. The reading level and associated characteristics of all children in the community.

2. A study one year later of *all the backward readers* in the community.

3. An analysis one year later of the difficulties of *all* children of *average intelligence* who continued to be *backward readers*; the terms 'backward reader' and 'average intelligence' being precisely defined for the purposes of this investigation in terms of the tests applied.

In 1966 an approach was made to the Scottish Education Department, with the request that it finance such a project over a 2-year period; while a further approach was made to the County of Dunbarton, in the West of Scotland, for permission for the study to take place in the schools in that area.

Chapter 2
Plan of Research

The County

The major portion of the County of Dunbarton lies along the
north side of the River Clyde adjacent to the City of Glasgow,
while a detached portion about a tenth of the total area is
situated a considerable distance from the rest of the county (see
Figure 1). As a whole the county is highly urbanized and industrialized in character, but it also contains some of the finest
scenery in Scotland in the Loch Lomond area. About 70 per cent
of the population live in the 2 large and 5 small burghs in the
county and in the new town of Cumbernauld, which is in the
'detached' area. The population of 215,765 in 1967 was nearly
11 per cent higher than the 1961 total. At the 1961 census more
than a quarter of the population was under the age of 15; this
proportion is also increasing.

When the present research commenced in session 1965–6,
26,367 primary pupils were enrolled in schools in the county
(age-range 5–12 years). Pupils in Roman Catholic schools
accounted for about one-third of the total, though this proportion was not evenly distributed throughout the county. There
were 69 primary schools or departments and 3 special schools
catering for this age-group. Fourteen of the primary schools were
small, with fewer than 7 teachers in each, that is less than one
teacher per age-group; while 23 were large, with more than 14
teachers. Eighteen schools (mostly large) were for Roman
Catholic children; the remainder were non-denominational
(see Figure 2).

All these particular local features made for their own particular
problems in provision of appropriate school accommodation
and adequate staffing, at a time when teacher shortage was
particularly severe and staff turnover a problem all over the
country. The county staffing of 824 primary teachers (790 women
and 34 men) was 56 short of the number required to fill vacancies

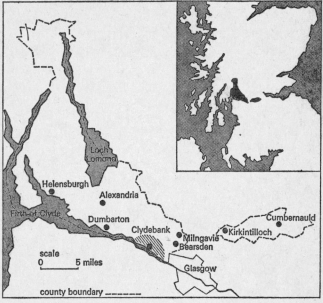

Figure 1 Map of Dunbartonshire

and remove over-size classes. Some primary schools had to contend with exceptionally large numbers of comparatively inexperienced teachers, and repeated changes of staff; staffing problems were particularly severe in the Roman Catholic schools. Almost a quarter of the women teachers were aged 25 or under, and married teachers constituted about 43 per cent of the total women teachers in the county. In both these categories the turnover of staff is very high.

In short, the environmental factors in the county pertinent to the present research are:

1. It is a highly industrialized area, with a number of large schools, but also a proportion of very small schools in outlying areas.

2. The area has a rapidly increasing population and increasing

proportion of school children.

3. There is a considerable and varying proportion of Roman Catholic children in separate schools. This proportion is also increasing.

4. As in other parts of Britain, there are many inexperienced teachers in the primary schools, which when combined with the high turnover of staff makes continuity of approach difficult to sustain.

5. There are over-size classes homogeneous for age, and smaller classes spanning a wider age-range in the rural districts.

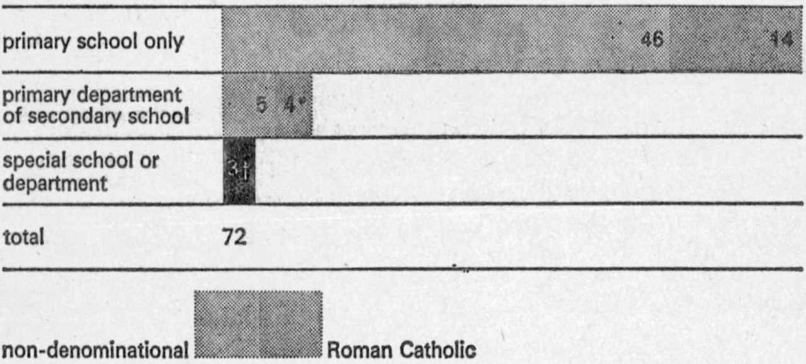

primary school only	46	14
primary department of secondary school	5 4*	
special school or department	3†	
total	72	

non-denominational ▓▓▓ Roman Catholic

*one of these schools is for boys only and one for girls only, all other schools are mixed

†one school is for the mentally handicapped, one for the mentally and physically handicapped, and one for the partially hearing

Figure 2   Types of School at Start of Study

In 1966 the County of Dunbarton had a primary-school population one-twentieth that of Scotland as a whole. There were in Scotland over 2,200 primary schools, but about half of these had a school roll of less than 100 pupils, while in a quarter of the schools there were fewer than 25 pupils. Yet one-fifth of the classes in Scotland had over 40 pupils. Dunbartonshire's problem with over-size classes and teacher shortage was about the national average. Thus in many ways the County of Dunbarton at the time of this research was facing, in the field of primary education, problems similar to those facing Scotland as a whole, and some of the results of this study have implications beyond the immediate area in which it took place. The extent to which generalizations are possible will be considered at a later stage.

The Sample

All schools with a primary department administered by the local authority in the County of Dunbarton were involved in the first stage of the project. Within the county there are primary schools with their own head teachers and also primary departments of secondary schools with an overall head of the two sections. There are no separate infant schools. Thus all children in the county can complete their primary schooling within a single school, that is, from five to twelve years of age. It is also possible for them to be transferred to a special school or department within the county, of which there are three.

A number of administrative changes took place in the county during the two years covered by the study, some of only minor significance so far as their effects on the organization of the research was concerned – for example, several of the primary departments attached to secondary schools became separate primary schools. Other changes caused greater difficulty; for example, the opening of a new school, to which was transferred part of the sample from one of the largest schools in the county.

The Age-Group

A request was sent in June 1966 to every school in the county which might contain children of the appropriate age, asking for the names, dates of birth and dates of commencing school of all children born in 1959 who were on the roll of the school on a given date in June 1966.

It seemed important in the study to equalize educational opportunity as far as possible, and at least as regards length of schooling. Two aspects of the educational organization in the county caused difficulty in adhering to this criterion:

1. Some schools had one intake per year in August; others had two, one in August plus another for which the date varied.

2. The age on admission varied markedly from school to school – the discrepancies being most marked between single and double entry-date schools.

Confining the sample to a given admission date would give a very wide age-range and was accordingly rejected; whereas confining the sample to those children whose date of birth fell within a limited part of the year – namely 1 April to 31 August 1959 – gave a group which was *homogeneous for length of schooling*, whether the child was in a one- or two-intake school, and whatever the limits set in a particular school for age on admission. Were the age-group extended even a month on either side this would no longer be true.

The reason for selecting these particular 5 months within a year has been indicated. The particular year of birth, 1959, was chosen in order that the children would come under observation at the point when they had completed 2 years of schooling. Seven years of age was as early as seemed appropriate to administer reading tests for screening purposes.

Size of Sample

The total number of children tested in the first screening stage of the research was 1544: 791 boys and 753 girls. No children were added to the sample if they entered the county after the given date, even if they were in the appropriate age-group; on the other hand children were withdrawn from the sample only if they left the county. Where they moved to schools *within* the county, they were tested in the school to which they transferred. Forty-three children (or 2·7 per cent) on the original list left the county during the first stage and were therefore not tested; while a further 43 changed schools *within* the county during the period of Stage 1, but were tested in the school to which they moved.

Some of the children attended very small schools with composite classes, while others attended schools with several classes per intake – 5·5 per cent of the sample were in schools with up to 10 children in the 5 months of the age-group tested; while 32·3 per cent were in schools with over 40 children in the sample (see Figure 3).

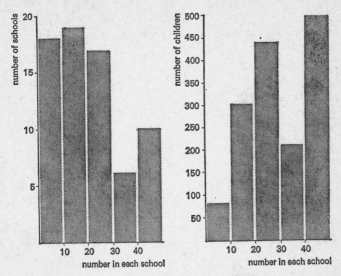

Figure 3 Distribution of Sample by Size of School at Start of Study

The Design

The investigation was planned to cover a 2-year period from October 1966 until June 1968, starting when the children had just completed 2 years of schooling. During that period all children in the schools in the county who met the criterion for selection at a particular stage were tested; only those who left the county escaped. A follow-up study and audiometric testing at the University of Strathclyde one year later, after the official completion of the study, included all but a minority of those who had been in the third phase of testing.

The plan of the research is shown in diagrammatic form in Figure 4, where the horizontal line at each stage represents reading level and the vertical line intelligence. Thus, the first phase of the study included all boys and girls in the schools in Dunbartonshire who had entered the county not later than June 1966 and had dates of birth between 1 April and 31 August 1959.

RESEARCH DESIGN

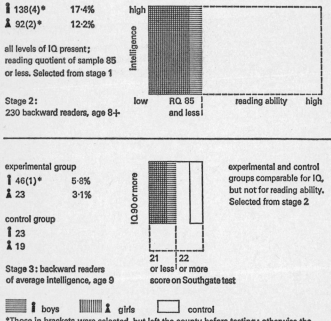

total	percentage of sample	
🯅 791	100	
🯅 753	100	

all levels of IQ and reading
ability present in sample

Stage 1: 1544 children, age 7+

🯅 138(4)*   17·4%
🯅 92(2)*   12·2%

all levels of IQ present;
reading quotient of sample 85
or less. Selected from stage 1

Stage 2:
230 backward readers, age 8+

experimental group
🯅 46(1)*   5·8%
🯅 23   3·1%

control group
🯅 23
🯅 19

experimental and control
groups comparable for IQ,
but not for reading ability.
Selected from stage 2

Stage 3: backward readers
of average intelligence, age 9

▬ 🯅 boys   ‖‖‖ 🯅 girls   ▢ control

*Those in brackets were selected, but left the county before testing; otherwise the
sample is complete at each stage

Figure 4 Research Design and Plan of Testing

PLAN OF TESTING

Criterion Reading Test	*Other Tests*	*Information*
Schonell Graded Word	EPVT (vocabulary) Laterality R–L differentiation Drawing	Absence Change of school in first 2 years

testing time: about half an hour per child

Southgate Reading Test 1	Daniels (spelling) WISC (intelligence) Adjustment questionnaire (completed by teacher)	Attendance Changes of school during third year Father's occupation

testing time: about two hours per child

Neale Analysis Accuracy and Comprehension	Diagnostic Reading Tests Auditory and visual discrimination R–L differentiation Motor co-ordination (Bender) ITPA on 69 of experimental group	Knowledge of letters and words Attitude to reading

testing time: about half a day per child

These 1544 children were tested individually over a 5-month period in the 70 schools they attended. The aim of this was to provide information on a total population for certain aspects of development with a possible relationship to reading level, and also so that a group of backward readers could be selected for further study. The second phase of the investigation, which was mainly in June 1967, was a further study of 14·9 per cent of the original population who had been regarded as 'at risk'. These 230 children were *all* the most backward readers (with reading quotient 85 or less), irrespective of intelligence. The aim of this second phase was to analyse the characteristics of a total group of backward readers, with information already available on the population from which they were drawn. On the basis of the results of this group on the second-stage testing, the third group was selected. For this final phase, the children were selected using a double criterion of low reading and average intelligence. These children, together with a control group who had also been at risk and were of similar intelligence but had improved in reading, were tested in the early part of 1968, when they were almost 9 years of age.

A summary of the information available on these groups of children is shown in Figure 4. Thus, on the total group of 1544 children, only the first-stage results are available, while for any group tested beyond that stage, any other results are in addition to those at the earlier stages.

For clarity of presentation, the three phases of the study – the population; the backward readers; and the continuing backward readers of average intelligence – will be discussed separately, preceded in each case by an outline of the testing. Only those tables necessary for understanding of the discussion will be included in the text; supplementary tables will be found in the appendix.

Part One
Reading in the Community at the Age of 7

Chapter 3
Testing for Stage 1

The preliminary testing, all of which was *individual* and untimed, was carried out between October 1966 and April 1967, when the children were 7+ and in their third year at school. It was carried out on *all* children in the selected age-group; that is, on 1544 children (791 boys and 753 girls). This testing was carried out by the author, a research assistant and about fifty students. All testers were given detailed briefing, including practice in scoring tests which were pre-recorded on video tape.

The tests used at this stage were all either tests which are available for administration by teachers, or simple screening devices requiring a minimum of training for their accurate administration. It was regarded as an essential part of the investigation that screening of the entire age-group should be undertaken, and that the group investigated should be sufficiently large to contain samples of the various types of anomaly under consideration. The problem was not the time taken in the actual testing, but the fact that the county covered a wide area, and that *all* children in the selected age-group were tested, which meant additional visits for absentees and for children who changed school.

Tests

The basic test used was the *Schonell Graded Word Reading Test* (Schonell and Schonell, 1960), a test of word recognition, giving scores in terms of total words correctly pronounced, this then being converted to a reading age for accuracy in reading isolated words out of context. This well-known test – which is not, however, the particular graded word test employed by the county psychologists in the area – was selected for this stage of the study as it was regarded as a useful, though rather crude, screening device. The reading ages on this were converted to reading quotients

$$\left(\frac{\text{reading age}}{\text{actual age}} \times 100\right)$$

in order to take account of the age differences at the time of testing.

The other main test employed was the *English Picture Vocabulary Test* (EPVT) by Brimer and Dunn (1963), which is a recently standardized British revision of the American *Peabody Picture Vocabulary Test*. Form 1 of this test was used, which covers the age-range 5 years to 8 years 11 months. This test was designed to assess levels of listening vocabulary, and can be administered irrespective of reading level. It is claimed that it 'gives information on the child's degree of verbal comprehension, which is diagnostically relevant to the understanding of reading difficulties and other verbal learning handicaps' (Brimer and Dunn, 1963, Manual, p. 1).

The test consists of 40 test items arranged in order of difficulty; each item is a page with 4 pictures and the task for the child is to identify the picture which is associated with a word spoken by the tester. The child can indicate by pointing to the appropriate picture. This test seemed more appropriate as a general test than would be a non-verbal test as a 'reading-free predictor of future language attainment' (Brimer and Dunn, 1963, Manual, p. 1).

The scores on EPVT are converted to standardized scores with a mean of 100 and standard deviation of 15.*

It was felt necessary to have a measure of the level of *motor coordination* for the complete sample against which to assess those who were screened out as being at risk. For this purpose all children in the sample were asked to copy a circle, a square and a diamond. The models which the children were asked to copy were similar to those in the *Stanford-Binet Intelligence Scale*,

---

*The *standard deviation* (SD) is the measure which indicates the extent to which the scores are clustered around the mean. If the standard deviation is small, scores are concentrated around the mean; if it is large, scores are more widely scattered. If the scores on a test are normally distributed, two-thirds of the scores will lie within one standard deviation on each side of the mean. In comparing the results of tests it is important to take into account both their means and standard deviations.

Form L-M (Terman and Merrill, 1961). Two attempts at each shape were given; the scoring standards were those in the Stanford-Binet, each attempt being scored separately, giving a maximum score of 6.

There has been so much controversy round the question of *laterality preferences* (of hand and eye) and their significance in reading (Clark, 1957, 1967), that in this area also it seemed important to have information for the total sample against which to assess the significance of the laterality preferences of those who were found to be having difficulty in reading. The child was asked to write his name on the record form, and the hand used for that and for drawing was noted. In addition, the child was asked to throw a paper ball into a basket. The hand used in each of three attempts at throwing was noted, as was the foot used in kicking the ball on each of three attempts. Eye preference was also noted. For this the child was given a piece of cardboard with a small hole in the centre, was asked to face the tester, holding the card in front of his eyes at arms' length and say how many fingers the tester was holding up. A note was made of the sighting eye, that is the one which could be seen through the hole. As it has recently been suggested that difficulty in discriminating right and left is of more significance in reading than laterality preference, an estimate was made for the whole sample of the level of ability to differentiate right and left. The instructions used were those used in the Isle of Wight Survey, though in that survey the children were from an older age-group.* One point was awarded for each correct response.

The tests of reading, listening, vocabulary, motor co-ordination, laterality, and ability to differentiate right and left were administered to the complete sample of 1544 children.

*The five instructions were as follows: (i) point to your nose with your left hand; (ii) point to your left ear with your right hand; (iii) point to my left hand (tester being opposite child); (iv) point to my right hand (tester's arms are crossed); (v) point to the wall on your left. The Isle of Wight Survey is reported in Rutter, Tizard and Whitmore (in press).

Additional Information

Information was collected on absence in each of the first 2 years of school, and any changes of school over the 2 years. Unfortunately it was not possible to collect this information at the time when the first testing was carried out, as some schools had reservations about permitting students access to record cards. As in data collected for a large sample such as this, there are a number of omissions; records were not always complete, and where the child had come from a school outside the county, the record card had in many instances not been forwarded.

Some of the larger schools had over 50 children in the sample, spread over a number of classes; under these circumstances it was felt that the maximum information which could legitimately be asked for the whole sample was absence-rate in each of the first 2 years at school, and changes of school during that time, as this information was available on all but a minority of the record cards. Any further information would needed to have come from other sources.

Chapter 4
Factors Related to Reading Level

One aim in surveying all children in the county born within the chosen 5 months was to provide normative data on a complete school population for a number of measures with a possible association with reading progress, against which clinic cases could be assessed. This chapter will be devoted to this aspect of the subject, preparatory to a more detailed analysis of those who were having difficulty with reading. The second aim was to select those children who were still having difficulty with the mechanics of reading at the age of 7, when reading was becoming necessary as a tool subject and when failure in reading would therefore lead to more general difficulty in achieving satisfactory progress in school. The criterion used was that any child should be further investigated if he failed to reach the level of reading necessary to tackle a simple book with which he was not familiar; this was equated with a reading quotient of 85 or less.

Reading Results

On the Schonell Graded Word Reading Test, a test of accuracy in reading words out of context, there was a slight tendency for the girls to score higher than the boys:

Boys – mean reading quotient: 106·8, standard deviation 20·9
Girls – mean reading quotient: 108·3, standard deviation 18·8
Total – mean reading quotient: 107·5, standard deviation 20

These results would also suggest that the children in this county were as a group scoring slightly *above* the norms for this test since, on the basis of the scoring method recommended by Schonell, the mean reading quotient expected would be 100. This was true both for the total group, and for the boys and girls considered separately. The norms for this test may be out of date and in need of revision, discussion of their appropriateness being, however, outside the brief for this research. These results come at a time when there is much discussion of a possible spiralling incidence of backwardness in reading, and the problems of increasing numbers of children entering the junior schools not having grasped the mechanics of reading (Gardner, 1968). Evidence that this is *not* the case in this county may be found here. In many areas in Scotland separate norms are used for word-recognition tests, not the norms currently in use in England, which tends to mask this fact. It was felt desirable in this present research to have a measure which could be compared with other areas, also because the 'real' measure being employed in selecting the 'at risk' sample was not reading age, but lack of independent reading skill. These remarks should not be taken as an attempt to minimize the problem of children who reached their third year at school without being able to read (even though in this county children did not change school at this stage); nor should they be taken as suggesting that the ideal *is* that all children should be reading fluently at this stage. Both these points, namely the appropriate action for assisting this group who are having difficulty, and a reduction in the size of the problem, require to be considered within the total educational scene. The tenor of the present argument is *not* that the ideal is necessarily for all children to reach a high level of mechanical reading ability as early as possible. In the present circumstances, where reading *is* expected of children beyond the age of 8, failure to reach this level must be regarded as serious, particularly in the light of studies such as those of Dr Joyce Morris (1966), who found that children who were having difficulty in reading at this age seldom recovered from this handicap.

This need for a minimum standard in reading within a few years of starting school is certainly not reduced by modern approaches, which perhaps even increase the need for independent study. Once a child has reached a certain level of reading competence, such reading tasks as are required by projects and the like may increase both his skill and his motivation. Below that level, requests to read to find out are more likely to cause frustration to the child, whose attempts to discover for himself will be baulked by his poor reading. Thus in present conditions the question is how to recognize these children early, and how most efficiently to prevent them from becoming educational outcasts. Clearly there is a need to ensure that such children *are* identified; and a need to ensure that class teachers teaching children beyond the age of 7 appreciate that they will have such children, and are equipped, with specialist guidance where necessary, to deal with them. This is *not* a problem which can be passed over to some other service, it is a classroom problem with which a teacher's professional training should equip her to deal. Isolated remedial tuition will never deal with this problem of the group of children who at a given point in time have not reached a predetermined standard. Flexibility in approach and a real understanding of the likely causative factors, combined with a thorough grasp of the appropriate methods of assisting a slow learner to reach a minimum standard, are required.

When the criterion of a reading quotient of 85 or less was used to select those who were, after 2 years at school, not yet beyond the earliest stages of learning to read, 236 children, or 15·3 per cent of the total group (18 per cent of boys and 12·5 per cent of girls), were brought into this category. Of these, 8 boys and 7 girls were unable to read any word on the Schonell Graded Word Reading Test. It should be remembered that *all* the poorest readers in the county are included in the sample, whether in a special school or not. Only one boy and one girl were, however, already in a special school at this stage. It must be stressed that the percentages quoted here, or in any large area, are in some ways a misleading statistic. The overall percentage of children in this county 'at risk' was about 15 per cent. However, this figure must not be taken to imply that in every school in the county about one child in six at that age will have difficulty in reading. Though the problem was present in most schools, its magnitude varied markedly from one school to another, and not in proportion to the size of school. Some of the causes of this variation lie in aspects of the school situation, others within the pre- and out-of-school environment mentioned in chapter 1. Each school has its own problems, some of which are unique; it can therefore be dangerous to make generalized statements or offer panaceas.

Perhaps an example would clarify this. If School A in a poor area, with a high incidence of backwardness in reading as the 'normal' feature, is faced with a child who is still having severe difficulty in coping with the initial stages of reading at the age of 8, necessary and appropriate measures would be very different from those in School B, in a district where the catchment area was such that usually there was little difficulty in ensuring that all children were reading with fluency and understanding at the age of 7. In School B, a child in difficulties with reading (even were his actual reading difficulty identical) would be under different and more severe pressures. This is the reason for concern at the possible misuse of normative data, which is a dangerous possibility with an extension of knowledge of assessment of attainment without parallel appreciation of the importance of diagnosis in the widest sense, a much more difficult concept.

Vocabulary Results

The results of the preliminary reading test given indicate that the level of attainment in the mechanical aspects of reading in the county was slightly above the Schonell norms both for boys and girls. One aim in using the EPVT was to provide some measure other than reading attainment against which the county as a whole could be assessed. No large-scale survey in Scotland has as yet utilized this test. The mean score on the test was established at 100, and standard deviation at 15. The mean score on the present sample of 1544 was 98·3, and standard deviation 11·7. On this test the boys scored slightly higher than the girls; the mean for boys was 100·1, for girls 96·5, which is similar to the finding in the standardization sample. To quote:

Whatever the explanation of the differences in favour of boys, it appears that the EPVTs are representing a characteristic vocabulary difference between the sexes, when this is assessed through oral administration. The differences are not attributable to accidental bias in the tests, but to differences in the function being measured (Brimer and Dunn, 1963, p. 32).

The school population in this study had an understanding

vocabulary below that of the group on which the EPVT was standardized. Thus, it cannot be deduced that any superiority in reading was the result of using a highly selected group of children. The value of this test as a predictor of the 'at risk' group will be considered later.

Relationship of Other Tests to Reading and Vocabulary Levels

The results of the other first-stage tests will be discussed briefly, and the possibility of an association with reading level considered. The percentages of children making each score will be shown in a table, as will be the mean reading quotients for children scoring at each level. A comparison will also be made between the trends for the reading and EPVT means; since trends which are present not only for reading but also for EPVT would not justify the hypothesis of an association specific to reading. To make this comparison between EPVT and reading within the various levels of score, it was necessary to re-scale the two tests so that their means and standard deviations were comparable. These comparisons are shown in a series of tables in the appendix, where both EPVT scores and reading quotients are shown to a mean of 100 and standard deviation of 15. In all other places the actual reading quotients are shown.

The Drawing Test

It may be remembered that the children were asked to draw a circle, a square and a diamond. Two attempts were allowed at each, with a maximum score of 6 if all were correctly drawn. Copying a circle correctly appears at the 3- year level on the Stanford-Binet Intelligence Scale, Form L-M; a square at the 5-year level; and a diamond at the 7-year level. Details of the results for the total group at the age of 7+ can be seen in Table 1, as can the mean reading quotients for each of the scores. Evidently, there was a tendency for the group of children with better motor co-ordination in this test to score higher in the reading test. This was true for both boys and girls. A similar trend was found on EPVT where those with high scores for drawing had also higher EPVT means (see Table A in appendix).

Table 1 Reading Level Related to Drawing ($n=1544$)

Score	Percentages			Mean reading quotient		
	boys	girls	all	boys	girls	all
6	10·7	7·8	9·3	115·5	117·2	116·2
5	23·3	21·7	22·5	112·6	115·5	114·0
4	37·0	38·5	37·8	106·9	108·2	107·5
3	18·1	21·5	19·7	98·8	105·3	102·3
2	10·9	10·5	10·7	98·5	93·1	95·9
Totals (%)	100	100	100	106·8	108·3	107·5

Ability to Differentiate Right and Left

Similar results were found here to those in the previous test (see Table 2). The group of children who were correct in all their responses in the test concerning right and left differentiation had a slightly higher mean reading quotient than those who failed this test. At this age only one-quarter of the children were able

Table 2 Reading Level Related to Ability to Differentiate Right and Left (*n*=1544)

Score	Percentages			Mean reading quotients		
	boys	*girls*	*all*	*boys*	*girls*	*all*
High 5	23·4	24·0	23·7	115·2	113·7	114·4
4	19·1	16·1	17·6	109·9	112·8	111·2
3	27·3	31·7	29·5	103·9	106·9	105·5
2	17·6	16·6	17·1	102·0	103·6	102·8
1	5·7	7·3	6·5	92·6	98·4	95·8
Low 0	6·9	4·3	5·6	105·8	105·8	105·0
Totals (%)	*100*	*100*	*100*	*106·8*	*108·3*	*107·5*

to answer these 5 questions correctly, while about 60 per cent made a score of 3 or less. Thus, such confusion *at that age* should not be regarded as clinically significant. Here also the pattern was similar for EPVT and reading quotient (see Table B in appendix).

Laterality Measures of Hand, Foot and Eye

An assessment was made of the child's hand preference, using writing hand as the criterion, throwing hand, and consistency in both measures. One test of eyedness was used, sighting with both eyes open. In footedness, kicking foot only was used as the criterion. In Table 3a the results of all these tests are shown for the total sample, and for boys and girls separately. Clearly, with regard to writing hand, the incidence of children using the left hand has increased, and there is now almost one child in ten of this age who is using his left hand for writing. The second important point is the marked sex difference shown here with regard to hand preference (10·9 per cent boys and 6·5 per cent girls left-handed). This sex difference was also shown in foot preference. There were a number of children for whom the preferred hand for throwing was not the same as that for writing. The proportion of children using the left eye was much higher, being about one in three, and here the proportions were similar in the two sexes. These findings are in accord with previous work in this field (Clark, 1957, 1959; Enstrom, 1962; Pringle, Butler and Davie, 1966).

In Table 3b the mean reading quotients for each of these categories are shown: not only reading quotients but also EPVT scores were similar for those with different laterality characteristics (see Table C in appendix).

In this study, even combining the data for the two sexes did not give evidence of a lower mean reading score in left-handers, those with mixed-handedness, or those who were left-eyed.

It is important to consider the sexes separately, since the incidence of left-handers is higher in boys, and the mean reading score of boys is lower, so that one might get an apparently lower mean reading quotient in left-handers not because there was a connexion, but because of the greater number of boys who were poor readers.

In the light of these findings it seems important that the following points be considered by anyone assessing the significance of laterality in cases of severe reading difficulty:

1. There was no evidence of difference in mean reading quotients between left- and right-handedness when the total population was considered, although there was a higher incidence of left-handedness in boys than in girls.

2. In any group of backward readers there is usually a higher proportion of boys than girls; thus a higher percentage of left-handedness would be expected even were there no connexion with reading progress. Thus the sexes must be considered separately and compared with incidence figures *for each sex*.

3. The more severe and prolonged the reading difficulty, the higher the proportion of boys in the sample. This is the finding in this

Table 3a Distribution of Laterality Characteristics in 1544 Children: Percentages of Right/Left/Mixed

	Boys			Girls			All		
	R	L	M	R	L	M	R	L	M
Writing hand	88·9	10·9	0·2	93·5	6·5	0	91·1	8·8	0·1
Writing and throwing	85·2	7·8	7·0	89·4	3·7	6·9	87·2	5·8	7·0
Preferred foot	85·1	11·0	3·9	91·6	3·9	4·5	88·3	7·5	4·2
Preferred eye	59·4	35·8	4·8	61·6	33·9	4·5	60·5	34·8	4·7

Table 3b Reading Level Related to Laterality (*n*=1544)

	Boys (106·8)			Girls (108·3)			All (107·5)		
	R	L	M	R	L	M	R	L	M
Writing hand	106·6	107·9	*	108·4	106·0	—	107·5	107·2	*
Writing and throwing	106·5	107·8	109·2	108·4	105·3	107·9	107·4	107·1	108·6
Preferred foot	106·7	107·9	103·7	108·4	107·2	106·8	107·6	107·7	105·3
Preferred eye	106·9	106·6	105·7	108·6	107·9	106·5	107·8	107·2	106·1

*Two cases only, 121·5

study, and in many others; and it emphasizes how misleading any general comparisons for the sexes combined can be.

4. The incidence of apparent left-handedness is increasing, so that any attempt to make comparisons using dated incidence figures for a population different in age or environment will again lead to unjustified conclusions.

5. There is a tendency to consider in a special category children who have reading difficulty *and* who are left-handed, and to refer them for special treatment. If any such selection is operating, clearly any incidence figures drawn from such a clinic population will be misleading. This is why this aspect of the study was regarded as important, since the first-stage population was large enough to justify the estimation of percentages in the different laterality categories, while in this second stage no criterion other than reading level was used in the selection.

Crossed laterality is the term used when a child's dominant or preferred hand and eye are on opposite sides. Taking writing hand as the criterion for handedness, 946 children had their dominant hand and eye on the same side (875 right, 71 left); 525 had their dominant eye on the opposite side (467 right hand, left eye and 58 left hand, right eye). The remaining 73 were mixed either for handedness or eyedness. Thus crossed laterality was no rare phenomenon and only 61 per cent of the group had their preferred hand and eye on the same side. Were the criterion preferred hand for writing *and* throwing on the same side, the proportion of the population with consistent laterality would have dropped even further. The more tests of eyedness or handedness, the smaller the proportion who would appear to be consistent. This is represented diagrammatically in Figure 5. The more tests of handedness or eyedness, the wider would be the 'doubtful' bands and therefore the greater the proportion either of 'crossed laterals' or of 'doubtful dominance'.

Here again, as in many other community studies, there was no evidence that left-handedness, left-eyedness, mixed dominance or crossed laterality were significant predictors of failure in reading (Stevenson and Robinson, 1953; Balow, 1963; Coleman and

Deutsch, 1964; Belmont and Birch, 1965; De Hirsch, Jansky and Langford, 1966; Douglas, Ross and Cooper, 1967).

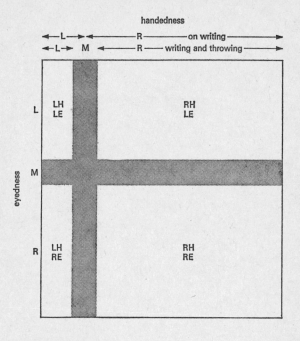

RH right-handed
LH left-handed
RE right-eyed
LE left-eyed
▨   mixed

Figure 5   Relationship of Handedness and Eyedness in the Group of 1544 Children (Illustrated Proportionately)

Absence

Information about absence was collected for the total group for each of their first 2 years at school. As can be seen in Table 4, there was a high absence-rate in the first year at school (with

Table 4 Reading Level Related to Absence from School in First 2 Years (*n*=1544)

Half-day absences	First year		Second year	
	percentage of children	mean RQ	percentage of children	mean RQ
0–20	29·1	109·0	35·6	110·1
21–40	27·3	108·7	30·6	108·2
41–80	28·7	107·7	24·5	104·9
81+	9·7	99·4	5·8	96·9
Not known	5·2	107·2	3·5	110·5
Totals (%)	*100*	*107·5*	*100*	*107·5*

38 ·4 per cent of the children absent at least one-tenth of the time). The rate was lower in the second year. There was no apparent sex difference in this distribution, and for this reason the sexes are combined in this table. There was evidence of a connexion between reading level and attendance, at least for those with a particularly high absence-rate. The effect of this was more marked in the second than in the first year. It would of course be surprising if there were no association between reading level and attendance! The records here were taken in retrospect, and only gross absence can be estimated from this; but as any teacher knows, the irregular attender is a greater problem than the child who has several long periods of absence in his first two years, say for infectious illnesses. This data was gathered mainly to provide incidence figures against which the records of the severely backward children could be discussed, and will therefore not be considered further here. However, not only reading but also EPVT scores varied with attendance level; though in this case the reading level was significantly affected, particularly by absence in the second year.

Changes of School

An interesting finding was the high proportion of children who either changed school within the county or moved into the county within their first 2 years at school; they made up about one-quarter of the sample (see Table 5). This is partly explicable by

Table 5 Reading Level Related to Changes of School in First 2 Years ($n=1544$)

	Percentage	*Mean R Q*
One school only	76·0	107·2
Two or more schools within county	11·5	107·6
From outside county	9·2	110·5
No record	3·3	106·2
Totals (%)	*100*	*107·5*

factors peculiar to this county at the time of the study. Mention was made earlier of the increase in the population in the county over the last few years, and in the proportion of the population of school age. Some of this apparent mobility within the county resulted from necessary administrative changes as a result of the apidly growing population. One of the reasons for the large number of children coming into the county is the rapid growth in the New Town of Cumbernauld, drawing its population from Glasgow. This development has meant both the absorption of large numbers of children from outside the county, and re-zoning within the new town as new schools have been built. The movement is no less real because it can be explained, and is a matter of concern both to teachers and to the children themselves. In many cases no records accompany the children who start school elsewhere, then enter the county within their first 2 years at school. Thus the new school knows nothing of the child's previous record of attendance, previous changes of school, to say nothing of approach to reading!

This fact of high mobility has important implications for the teaching of reading. It would be no solution to standardize the approach to the early teaching of reading in an area within the county, since there is as much mobility from outside the county. Awareness of a variety of approaches and flexibility in adjusting to the needs of incomers to the school, whether they be from another school in the county or from further afield, seems important. Evidence that the Dunbartonshire teachers must have this in a certain measure is to be seen from the fact that there was no evidence of lower mean reading scores in those who had been at two schools compared with those who had attended only one. It should be noted in connexion with the slightly higher reading level of those children who came from outside the county that they were also above the rest of the group on the EPVT (see Table E in appendix).

Clearly, the strongest association with reading in these first stage tests is that of the EPVT. The variations in mean reading scores which do occur with different levels of ability in drawing, and ability to differentiate right and left, are similar to the variations in EPVT; while in the laterality tests there is evidence of little variation in the means *on either measure*. Only when absence is considered is there any evidence of a trend specific to reading. Before discussing the results of the group of backward readers on the second-stage testing, their results on the above tests will be considered separately.

Part Two
Backward Readers at the Age of 8

Chapter 5
Testing for Stage 2

All children who were regarded as 'at risk' and therefore selected for further study had a reading quotient of 85 or less on the Schonell Graded Word Reading Test, that is, after 2 years at school they were still unable to tackle even a simple book unaided. There were 236 children (or 15·3 per cent of the sample) who were in this category. All but the 6 who left were included for further study; and none of these 6 was either severely backward or of high EPVT score (the highest boy scored 96 and the highest girl 78). A comparison of the backward readers and the total sample, for the two sexes separately, may be seen in Figure 6. Only 8 girls at risk scored 100 or above on EPVT; while 30 of 138 boys scored 100 or above. The mean EPVT score for this group was 87·6, standard deviation 11·8. 'At risk' girls formed a smaller, *and* a duller group (boys' mean 90·2, standard deviation 11·2; girls' mean 83·7, standard deviation 11·8). This was confirmed on the Wechsler Intelligence Scale for Children (see pp. 63–8).

There was some evidence that these children were also poor in motor co-ordination, as measured by the drawing test. This result could be misleading, since the finding was more clear-cut with the girls than the boys, and is, to some extent, explicable in terms of their lower level of general intelligence. This particular task features in an intelligence test; it is, nevertheless, worth mentioning, as indicating that in some backward readers their deficit is not specific to the area of spoken language. Fewer of the backward readers were able to differentiate right and left; but it should be noted that 12 per cent of them made a perfect score. The proportion of the backward readers who had moved school in the first 2 years was similar to that in the total group. Twenty-five of them had at least one change of school in their third year – at a time when they were still having difficulty with reading. At a time when it was becoming a necessary tool they moved to a school where their background was not known and their difficulties might not immediately be appreciated. The absence-rate in the whole population was high in the first year at school, but lower in the second year. For some of this group of backward readers the absence-rate continued to be high in the second and even third year. But here again there were children whose attendance was regular.

The Sample: Stage 2

The number of children tested at this stage of the investigation was 230 (138 boys and 92 girls), or 14·9 per cent of the original sample. Those who left the county were lost to the study, but, as in the first stage, those who moved within the county were tested in their new schools. It should be remembered that *all* the poorest readers in the county are included in this sample, whether or not they were in a special school for the mentally handicapped.

Tests

All children in this group were tested individually, or in groups of two or three, on the *Southgate Reading Test 1*, which is a 30-item test involving selection of the appropriate word from 5 alternatives in response to a spoken word (Southgate, 1958). The *Daniels Spelling Test*, a 40-item test of words graded in difficulty from simple regular words to more complicated irregular ones ('on' to 'beautiful'), was administered on the same occasion (Daniels and Diack, 1958). All children were tested on reading and spelling as near as possible to the end of their third year at school.

These children were also all tested on the *Wechsler Intelligence Scale for Children* (Wechsler, 1949).* No child was tested on WISC until he had reached his eighth birthday (age-range on testing 8 years to 8 years 5 months). This meant that all children were tested on the same coding test. In the literature on children

---

*Since the Scottish standardization was used, only the following sub-tests could be used: *verbal* – information; comprehension; arithmetic; similarities and vocabulary; *performance* – picture completion; picture arrangement; block design; object assembly and coding.

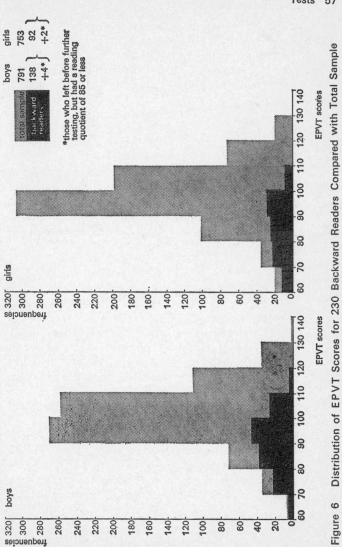

Figure 6 Distribution of EPVT Scores for 230 Backward Readers Compared with Total Sample

suffering from severe reading disability there has been a great deal of discussion on both the relative levels in verbal and performance tests of intelligence, and on the possibility of particular sub-groups of children with severe reading difficulty categorized by the verbal/performance pattern. The significance of high or low scores on specific sub-tests has also been considered in a number of studies. Here, also, there is little agreement. A number of the studies have a very wide age-range, limited numbers, unequal numbers of the two sexes, a biased sample or vague definition of reading disability.* For this reason it seemed important to secure this data for the whole backward population; otherwise a quick screening for intelligence could have been undertaken at an earlier stage, and a test such as the WISC used only for the final stage of the study. Once the WISC was chosen as the most appropriate criterion for intelligence, and as a tool for discrimination within that concept, this determined the earliest moment at which it could appropriately be applied. From evidence gained in the course of the Scottish standardization of the WISC, it was clear that discrimination between sub-test scores could not justifiably be made with children under the age of 8. Unfortunately the WPPSI (Wechsler Pre-school and Primary Scale for Intelligence), the downward extension of the WISC, was not available in Britain at the time of this investigation, otherwise such an extension would have permitted a discrimination of this kind to be made at an earlier age.

Additional Information

Information on absence and changes of school during the third year was obtained for this group, though not for the whole sample; the father's occupation was also noted. This latter proved a more difficult task than was anticipated, as it was entered in only a proportion of the record cards; and even then it was, of course, three years out of date. It was possible in some instances that the father might now be unemployed, and in others that there might be no male head of the household. Where possible the informa-

* See Belmont and Birch (1966) for a critical analysis of such studies.

tion was confirmed, and where there was no information on the card the teacher attempted to obtain it. In view of the possible sources of unreliability of this information, it was used only to give a rough estimate of social class according to a modification of the Registrar-General's classification. Information on adjustment in school was obtained with the assistance of the class teachers, who completed the *Rutter Child Scale* for all the 'at-risk' sample.* This questionnaire, which gives a total score for adjustment, and a separate neuroticism and anti-social score, has been used recently in a community study in the Isle of Wight, and a study made of the association between different scores on this test and reading level. For this reason, combined with the fact that the results on it have been compared in the Isle of Wight survey with those obtained from parental questionnaires, and psychiatric interview, it seemed a useful instrument, providing as it does comparative data. All three scores were noted, and special attention was paid to whether the teachers scored positively the items on speech defects, since these also had been noted in children with severe reading difficulty.

* The kindness of Dr Rutter in permitting the use of the Child Scale, and also providing the printed copies of the test for the purpose, is greatly appreciated. See Rutter (1967) for details of the scale.

Chapter 6
Spelling, Intelligence and Adjustment in Relation to Reading

Reading

The Southgate Reading Test requires only the ability to select and circle from 5 printed words the one appropriate to the picture and spoken by the tester; several items do not have a picture, and here the child is dependent on the spoken word. As can be seen from Table 6, at the end of 3 years at school there was still in the schools the problem of children who were unable to perform even such a simple reading task. Half of this group scored 21 or less on the test, which on the test norms is a reading age of 7 years or less. Of these, only 6 were in a special school (4 boys and 2 girls), while the one remaining child in a special school scored over 21. It is felt that all these 120 children were still without adequate reading skill for the simplest classroom needs – they were now 8 years of age, and the problem could neither be solved by retaining them in the infant department nor by sending them all to a special school.

Table 6   Reading Scores and Reading Ages of 230 Backward Readers on Southgate Test at 8 Years of Age

	Score of 21 or less			Score of 22 or more		
Scores	0–6	7–11	12–21	22–25	26–30	
Reading ages*	6 or less	6·1–6·6	6·7–7	7·1–7·6	7·7 or more	Totals
Boys	4	14	51	40	29	138
Girls	3	10	38	24	17	92
All	7	24	89	64	46	230
Totals	120			110		230

*Reading ages in years and months.

Spelling

The Daniels Spelling Test is a 40-item test with words ranging in difficulty from 'on' to 'beautiful'; the first 10 words are simple 2- and 3-letter phonetically regular words ('on' to 'beg'). As can be seen from Table 7, 59 children, or one-quarter of this group, could not write 10 simple words correctly. In terms of a class-room problem this represents about 4 per cent of the original population studied. Clearly this is not a problem which can be passed over to some outside agency. In this connexion the work of Margaret Peters in *Spelling: Caught or Taught?* (1967) seems pertinent; she emphasizes the important role of the teacher in affecting progress in learning to spell and the need for a con-structively planned programme of spelling geared to each child's individual needs.

Table 7 Spelling Scores and Spelling Ages of 230 Backward Readers on Daniels Test at 8 Years of Age

Spelling ages*	Scores 0–9		Scores 10–18		Scores 19–31		Totals
	0 Non-speller	1–9 6 or less	10–14 6·1– 6·6	15–18 6·7– 7·0	19–26 7·1– 8·0	27–31 8·1 and over	
Boys	8	30	20	32	42	6	138
Girls	2	19	23	11	33	4	92
All	10	49	43	43	75	10	230
Totals	59		86		85		230

*Spelling ages in years and months.

An analysis was made of the reversal errors on the spelling test within this total group of backward readers, in order to have some idea of how common this phenomenon is in children at this level of reading. An analysis was made of the numbers of reversed or inverted letters, e.g. 'd' for 'b' or 'p', and the number of words where the letter order was reversed, e.g. 'geb' for 'beg'. Table 8 shows that such results were found in almost half such a group (2 were non-writers, and the writing of 26 illegible, which meant that no assessment could be made; of the remainder only 94, or 40·9 per cent, had no reversals). In short it is a common phenomenon. Reversals were commoner in those with lower reading level; only one-quarter of those with Southgate score of 21 or less were legible writers with no reversals. Thus, when seeing children in a clinic whose reading age is below 7 years, such reversal errors are the rule rather than the exception.

Table 8 Incidence of Reversal Errors in 230 Backward Readers by Reading Level, Intelligence and Sex at 8 Years of Age

Categories of error	Reading* 21−	22+	Intelligence† 90−	90+	Sex boys	girls	Frequencies	%
No faults	31	63	16	78	59	35	94	40·9
Reversals, etc.	61	47	29	79	61	47	108	46·9
Illegible	26	—	14	12	17	9	26	11·3
Non-writer	2	—	2	—	1	1	2	0·9
Totals	120	110	61	169	138	92	230	100

*Reading by Southgate test: 90− means that full scale, verbal and performance were all below 90.
†Intelligence by WISC.

An analysis of the writing of this group was also made, using the spelling test scripts. Admittedly there was a danger that such an assessment would be contaminated by awareness of spelling errors. Every effort was made to avoid this, and two judges were used. It seemed more realistic to use, for the assessment, writing used in a normal task rather than writing produced solely for that purpose, as writing is employed in this way as a tool. As can be seen, two of these children were non-writers, while 21 were considered very bad, and 114 poor. The results were similar for the two sexes. When these were analysed by reading level it was found that only one of those whose writing had been rated as very bad had a Southgate score of over 21; while 13 of them had no IQ above 90, the remaining 8 had at least one IQ above 90. The analysis of quality of writing is shown in Table 9, both by reading and intelligence level.

Table 9 Quality of Writing in 230 Backward Readers by Reading Level, Intelligence and Sex at 8 Years of Age

Quality of writing	Reading* 21−	22+	Intelligence† 90−	90+	Sex boys	girls	Frequencies	%
Good	3	11	0	14	8	6	14	6·1
Not so good	34	45	11	68	46	33	79	34·3
Poor	61	53	35	79	69	45	114	49·6
Very bad	20	1	13	8	14	7	21	9·1
Non-writer	2	—	2	—	1	1	2	0·9
Totals	120	110	61	169	138	92	230	100

*Reading by Southgate test.
†Intelligence by W I S C.

Intelligence

All children in the 'at risk' group were tested on the WISC and the age-range on testing was 8 years to 8 years 5 months. Thus, the sample on which these results are based was large, and homogeneous both for age and locality; it was in fact as large as the test standardization sample of the same age-group. Even with the assistance of the Scottish standardization which was used here, a number of verbal responses were found to provide ambiguities in scoring (Scottish Council for Research in Education, 1965). The necessity for approaching with caution any analysis of WISC results with young children was clearly brought out in this study, as was the need for agreed scoring on ambiguous items. With this age-group it was possible for a change of only one point in raw score on a single sub-test to affect the full scale I Q by several points. The new Wechsler Pre-School and Primary Scale of Intelligence (WPPSI) (Wechsler, 1963), which is now available in Britain as well as in the United States, does not wholly solve this problem. Though it does overlap with the WISC, it can only be used up to the age of 6 years 3 months, thus still leaving a gap of 2 years in the practicable use for diagnostic purposes of an otherwise continuous scale.

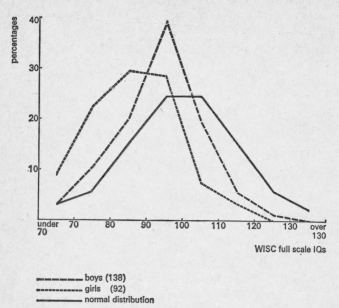

boys (138)
girls   (92)
normal distribution

Figure 7 Intelligence of 230 Backward Readers (Age-Range on Testing 8 to 8 Years 5 Months) Compared with the Normal Distribution on WISC

The distribution of intelligence in this sample of 230 backward readers may be seen in Figure 7, where boys and girls are shown separately, as is the normal distribution of full scale IQ on this test. The mean full scale IQ for the total group was 89·8, standard deviation 11·9 (boys 92·8, standard deviation 11 and girls 85·3, standard deviation 11·9). Thus, not only were more boys found to be 'at risk', but also their distribution of intelligence was more nearly normal than that of the girls. This pattern was repeated in the sub-test scores for the two sexes, where a profile for the two sexes ran parallel, but with the boys scoring above the girls (see Figure 8). Neither sex had specifically low scores in any particular sub-tests. The mean verbal IQ was lower than the performance IQ in both sexes (mean verbal IQ 89·5, standard deviation 11·4, mean performance IQ 93·4, standard deviation

13·1 – see Table F in appendix for full details). When the verbal performance discrepancy, or difference between the two scales, was considered, it was found that the proportion of children scoring markedly different verbal and performance I Qs was no different from that found in a normal sample, where it can be

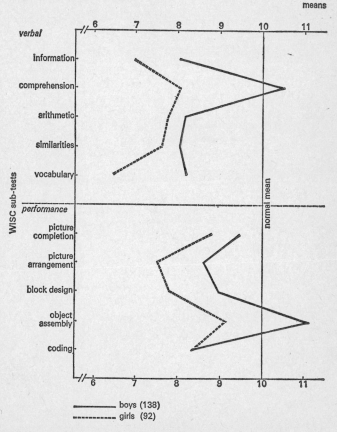

Figure 8 Mean Scores on W I S C Sub-Tests for 230 Backward Readers (Age-Range on Testing 8 to 8 Years 5 Months)

expected that 54·9 per cent will have a difference of 9 points
or more.* Where the difference lay in this group was in the
distribution of these widely discrepant results, as may be seen
from Table 10. Instead of being equally distributed between

Table 10 Difference between Verbal and Performance Levels on
WISC for 230 Backward Readers (Age 8 to 8 Years 5 Months)

	Discrepancy in points	Boys	Girls	Total	
Verbal IQ higher	20	1	—	1	
	15–19	9	—	9	25 *(10·9%)*
	10–14	5	10	15	
+	1–9	30	23	53	
Verbal and performance IQ					134 *(58·3%)**
the same	0	7	—	7	
—	1–9	43	31	74	
Performance IQ higher	10–14	23	11	34	
	15–19	15	8	23	
					71 *(30·8%)*
	20–24	5	4	9	
	25–29	—	5	5	
Totals		*138*	*92*	*230*	

* 54·9% of Scottish standardization sample had up to 9 points
difference.

verbal higher and performance higher, here, on the contrary, far
more children had a higher performance score. Thus the full
scale IQ in these children was being inflated by the performance
side of the test in comparison with their verbal ability.

The extent to which children of different levels of intelligence
were appearing in this sample may be seen from Table 11; that
is, children who were found to be having difficulty with the
mechanics of reading after 2 years at school. It is also possible

*See Scottish Council for Research in Education (1967).

Table 11 Comparison of Reading and Intelligence in 230 Backward Readers at 8 Years of Age

Intelligence on WISC	Reading						Total	% of 230
	Southgate score 21—			Southgate score 22+				
	boys	girls	all	boys	girls	all		
Full IQ								
100 and over	9	5	14	28	5	33	47	20·4
90–99	28	8	36	27	18	45	81	35·2
under 90*	32	38	70	14	18	32	102	44·4
Totals	*69*	*51*	*120*	*69*	*41*	*110*	*230*	*100*
Verbal IQ								
100 and over	11	4	15	25	7	32	47	20·4
90–99	22	5	27	24	15	39	66	28·7
under 90*	36	42	78	20	19	39	117	50·9
Totals	*69*	*51*	*120*	*69*	*41*	*110*	*230*	*100*
Performance IQ								
100 and over	18	7	25	39	10	49	74	32·2
90–99	24	15	39	20	20	40	79	34·3
under 90*	27	29	56	10	11	21	77	33·5
Totals	*69*	*51*	*120*	*69*	*41*	*110*	*230*	*100*

*In a normal population 50% of children would be expected to have an IQ between 90 and 109, and 25% of the remainder would have an IQ under 90.

from the table to contrast the intelligence levels of this group when re-tested after 3 years at school on the Southgate test, since those with a score of 21 or less (reading age 7 years or less) are shown separately from those scoring 22 to 30 on this test. Two points clearly emerge. First, only a limited proportion of those who were initially at risk were of average intelligence, and the proportion was still lower if verbal score was the criterion rather than performance score. Second, an analysis of the group on testing at 8 years of age indicates that within the total 'at risk' group those whose difficulty was severe and continued were more likely to be of low intelligence. A further reading test was carried out one year later on all but those with extremely low intelligence, and the results of this test may be seen on page 80.

Reading and spelling are not of course independent variables; thus the scores on the spelling test would be adversely affected where a child was still having difficulty with reading. It is possible, however, that some children no longer severely backward in reading might still be failing in spelling. In Table 12 the different spelling results related to levels of intelligence are shown. Here again it is evident that few children of average intelligence had failed to learn how to spell simple words by the age of 8; and most of those who had failed were boys.

Social Class Distribution

As indicated earlier, the information concerning parents' occupation on which the social class distribution was based was incomplete and also suspect in a number of instances. It is likely to err on the favourable rather than the unfavourable side. Where the record was incomplete, necessitating seeking out the information at the time of the study, it was in fact more up to date, for example, as to whether the father was employed or whether there was a male head of the house. Also, on some of the record cards the father's occupation was described in terms preferred by the parent. In Figure 9 the social class distribution is shown. Twenty of the children had fathers who were unemployed, while at least another 12 had no male head of the house.

Adjustment

It seemed important that the questionnaire used to assess the behaviour of the backward readers be not only valid and reliable but also that it be short and appear meaningful to the teachers completing it. The questionnaire recently developed by Dr Michael Rutter (1967), for the age-range 7 to 13 years, seemed to meet these requirements. His questionnaire has been used with Aberdeen children, in the Isle of Wight, and with clinical cases attending the Maudsley Hospital in London. In the Isle of Wight

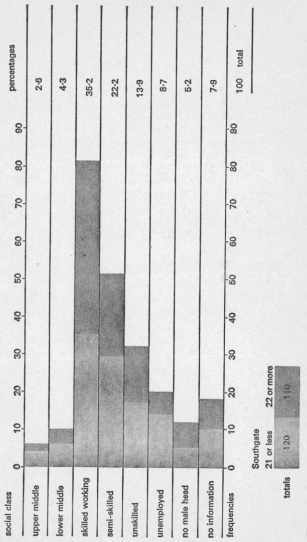

Figure 9 Social Class of Backward Readers in Relation to Reading Level

Table 12 Comparison of Spelling and Intelligence in 230 Backward Readers at 8 Years of Age

Intelligence on WISC	Spelling age on Daniels test									Total % of 230
	6 and under			6·1–7·0			7·1 and above			
	boys	girls	all	boys	girls	all	boys	girls	all	
Full IQ										
100 and over	3	1	4	14	4	18	20	5	25	47 20·4
90–99	13	3	16	23	7	30	19	16	35	81 35·2
under 90*	22	17	39	15	23	38	9	16	25	102 44·4
Totals	38	21	59	52	34	86	48	37	85	230 100
Verbal IQ										
100 and over	2	1	3	16	3	19	18	7	25	47 20·4
90–99	11	2	13	19	5	24	16	13	29	66 28·7
under 90*	25	18	43	17	26	43	14	17	31	117 50·9
Totals	38	21	59	52	34	86	48	37	85	230 100
Performance IQ										
100 and over	9	1	10	20	8	28	28	8	36	74 32·2
90–99	11	6	17	21	11	32	12	18	30	79 34·3
under 90*	18	14	32	11	15	26	8	11	19	77 33·5
Totals	38	21	59	52	34	86	48	37	85	230 100

* In a normal population 50 % of children would be expected to have an IQ between 90 and 109, and 25 % of remainder would have an IQ under 90.

study another behaviour questionnaire was also used – one completed by parents – and a comparison made between the two. Psychiatric interviews were also employed and their results compared with both questionnaires.

The scale has 26 items concerning the child's behaviour, and the teacher is asked for each to indicate whether it 'certainly applies', 'applies somewhat' or 'doesn't apply'. These indications are scored as 2, 1 or 0 respectively, and a total score is then obtained for each child. In addition, the scores for certain items are grouped together to obtain a neurotic sub-score (items such as 'often worried', 'unhappy', 'tearful', etc.), and an anti-social sub-score (for items such as 'often tells lies', 'is often disobedient', 'bullies other children', etc.). A score of 9 points or more on the total scale is considered to show evidence of some disorder. For children with such a score a comparison is then made between their scores on the neurotic and the anti-social items.

All 3 scores were calculated for this group of children, and a note made of cases where the teacher marked positively the 2 items concerning speech defect.

1. In this sample of 228 backward readers (2 children left the county and the questionnaire was not returned), 64 boys and 45 girls made such a score of 9 or more, indicating some disorder; this is approximately equal proportions of boys and girls, and comprises 47·4 per cent of the group of backward readers.

In Rutter's studies 11 per cent of boys and 3·5 per cent of girls in the general population, and 80 per cent of boys and 60 per cent of girls in a clinic sample, had such scores. He also found a raised incidence of disorder in his backward readers as compared with his control group, not only as assessed by the teachers but also as assessed by their parents, evidence that their abnormal behaviour was not only found in the classroom situation. This, of course, does not indicate the extent to which the maladjustment was causal or was a result of the reading, since neither in Rutter's studies nor in the present investigation was the questionnaire completed before the child's difficulty with reading was evident. Some of the other evidence in that investigation, however, led them to suspect that the reading difficulties might be the primary cause, and the anti-social behaviour a reaction to that. The incidence of maladjustment in this sample was slightly higher than in the Isle of Wight survey, but this could be the result of the inclusion in this study of children of lower intelligence than those in the Isle of Wight study. The results are shown in Table 13, divided by reading and intelligence levels, and they indicate that there was slightly more maladjustment noted both in the poor readers and those of lower intelligence.

Table 13 Adjustment in 230 Backward Readers Aged 8 Years, as Assessed by Teachers

Questionnaire score	Reading		Intelligence		Sex		Frequen-cies	%
	21—	22+	90—	90+	boys	girls		
9 or more*	68	41	38	71	64	45	109	47·4
Less than 9	51	68	22	97	73	46	119	51·7
No questionnaire	1	1	1	1	1	1	2	0·9
Totals	120	110	61	169	138	92	230	100

*A score of 9 or more is taken to indicate some disorder.

2. These children with a total score of 9 or more, regarded as having some disorder, are considered to determine whether this is preponderantly neurotic or anti-social. Where the two sub-scores are the same, they remain undifferentiated. Rutter found that in his control group the numbers high on the neurotic and anti-social measures were comparable; while in his backward readers (aged 9 to 10 years), though both measures showed a raised incidence, anti-social was twice as common (23·3 per cent anti-social and 12·8 per cent neurotic). A similar pattern was found in this present study (see Table 14). Rutter also found more boys than girls were rated as anti-social.

3. Two items on the questionnaire were concerned with speech defects. Speech defect was scored positively for 27·8 per cent of the backward readers. (For further details see Table 15.)

It is not possible to take the comparison with the Isle of Wight investigation further in this present report, as this would neces-

Table 14 Type of Maladjustment in Backward Readers Aged 8 Years, as Assessed by Teachers*

	Frequencies			Percentages		
	boys	girls	all	boys	girls	all
Anti-social	35	25	60	54·7	55·5	55·1
Neurotic	24	17	41	37·5	37·8	37·6
Undifferentiated	5	3	8	7·8	6·7	7·3
Totals	64	45	109	100	100	100

* Only those who scored 9 points or more on the questionnaire are included in this table. 'Undifferentiated' are those whose anti-social and neurotic scores were equal.

sitate a detailed discussion of the composition of the groups of backward readers in the two studies, since the criteria for selection were different. The results are in line with the general results

Table 15 Incidence of Speech Defect as Reported by Teachers in 230 Children Aged 8 Years, by Reading Level, Intelligence and Sex*

	Reading†		Intelligence†		Sex		Frequen-cies	%
	21—	22+	90—	90+	boys	girls		
Speech defect reported	39	25	17	47	45	19	64	27·8
None reported	80	84	43	121	92	72	164	71·3
No question-naire	1		1	1	1	1	2	0·9
Totals	120	110	61	169	138	92	230	100

*Only those with at least one IQ 90 + were tested again on reading at 9 years of age. Forty-seven children had at least one IQ 90 + and speech defect reported at the age of 8. Ten of these were in 19 worst readers at the age of 9 (see Table 16).
† Reading by Southgate test; intelligence by WISC.

of the Isle of Wight survey, both in finding a higher incidence of maladjustment in backward readers and proportionately greater anti-social as compared with neurotic symptoms, as assessed by teachers. A detailed analysis of the relationship between maladjustment and reading progress is to be found in the Isle of Wight survey (Rutter, Tizard and Whitmore, in press). In a number of other ways the two researches also showed similar results, with slightly lowered intelligence in the backward readers, difficulty in differentiating right and left, and evidence of speech defect in many of the backward readers, together with a lack of association with left- or mixed-handedness. One in six of the backward readers in the Isle of Wight survey still showed abnormalities of articulation even at the age of 9 to 10 years.

These results indicate that most children in this county had mastered the mechanics of reading by the age of 8 years, and grasped sound symbol association well enough to be able to write regularly spelt words correctly. A problem remained for the schools, and this was how to deal with the children who had still not mastered these skills by the age of 8. It would appear unlikely that they could now be catered for within the classroom, and would require some specialist assistance in order to help them to acquire the skills. This was, however, clearly a difficulty which was mainly confined to children of lower than average intelligence and to children who came from the lower end of the social class distribution. The problem was *not* how to deal with a group of highly intelligent children who had failed to learn to read and spell. Relatively few intelligent children remained a severe risk; though some had been slow in starting, most *had* grasped the mechanics of reading by the age of 8. The task of teaching them to read was not over, but was now a matter rather of developing a facility in reading with understanding in a manner appropriate to different types of reading material. They had now reached a level where a wide range of attractive books on their reading level and appropriate to their interests would help to provide the motivation which would carry them forward towards developing higher reading skills. A study of this aspect of reading instruction was not the aim of this research. Its aim was to consider those with continuing, severe reading difficulty. Until this point, no child has been excluded by virtue of his intelligence, the only criterion for exclusion having been satisfactory reading level. The remainder of the book will be concerned with a study in depth of those children who in spite of at least one score on the intelligence test within the normal range were still, at the age of 8, having difficulty with the mechanics of reading. A comparison with others in the original sample of backward readers who were no longer having such severe problems will also be made.

Part Three
Prolonged Reading Difficulty in Children of Average Intelligence

Chapter 7
The Extent of Reading Difficulty

The results discussed so far have been either of all children of the selected age in the county or of all backward readers within that group. The children who will be considered now are almost 9 years of age, and all have at least one score on the WISC which is within the average range. So far, it has been shown that a number of such children were at risk when the study began; and some were still potential cases of severe reading disability after 3 years at school. What is their position now?

All children who had been selected originally as backward readers, who were still in the county, and who were of 'average' intelligence (as defined in this study), were tested on the *Neale Analysis of Reading Ability* (Neale, 1966), on which the child is asked to read aloud a series of passages graded in difficulty, and after each passage is asked some questions to test his understanding of what he has read. On the basis of this, reading ages for accuracy and for comprehension are calculated. A reading age of 7 years or less on that test means in 'real' terms that the child in question still has difficulty in reading a very simple short passage with understanding, while making only minor errors, while with a reading age of 8 years he would manage to grasp the meaning and make few errors in a relatively easy reading task. A child with a reading age at the 7-year level would be able to read the following passage with only minor errors:

> A little boy came to see me.
> He left his ball at my house.
> Then he went away.
> Now I play with it myself.

There were 165 children (106 boys and 59 girls) who had originally been backward readers and who were of average intelligence. In Table 16 details of the accuracy scores for this complete group

Table 16   Neale Accuracy Score in Relation to IQ on WISC

IQ level on WISC	Neale reading ages												Totals
	No score		7 and under		7·1–8·0		8·1–9·0		Over 9		
	boys	girls	boys	girls	boys	girls	boys	girls	boys	girls	
All IQs 100 or above*	–	–	1	–	11	3	10	3	4	–	
At least one IQ 100+*	–	–	4	–	31	12	23	8	6	2	
All IQs 90 or above*	1	–	7	–	32	13	24	8	6	4	
At least one IQ 90+	2	2	13	2	47	33	34	15	10	7	165
No IQ 90 or above											61
Left county											4
Total 'at risk' group											230

*These lines are not additive, but different criteria.
Note: Table includes all of the backward readers, at age of 9, who had any IQ 90 or above on WISC.

of children are shown. The comprehension score is not independent of the accuracy score, since testing is stopped once the child
reaches a certain error level. However, the trend on the comprehension results was similar to that for accuracy. Three points
clearly emerged:

1. The lower the level of intelligence within the group the greater
the likelihood that the child will still have difficulty with reading,
whether comprehension or accuracy is under consideration.

2. The risk of continued severe difficulty in reading is greater for
a boy than for a girl. Furthermore, a girl is unlikely to have
continued difficulty, unless she is also of low intelligence.

3. The incidence of continued severe reading disability in children
of average intelligence in this county was not as high as many
other reports would have led one to anticipate. These children
were about 9 years of age at the time of this testing; thus
taking a reading age of 7 years or less, or 2 years or more backward in reading, as the criterion for severe reading disability,
there were *15 boys* and *4 girls* who met that criterion.

At this stage it is worth drawing attention to the relative size of
the community problem of children with 'average' intelligence
who at the age of 9 years were still found to be severely backward
in reading *for whatever cause*. In the county studied in this
investigation, the maximum size of this problem at the severe
level of 2 or more years backward was $1 \cdot 2$ per cent of the total
population of this age, most of these being boys; while another
$5 \cdot 1$ per cent were moderately backward, that is between one and
two years behind the level expected on that test for children of
their age. These percentages include *all* children with at least one
IQ of 90 or above whatever the cause of their slow progress,
provided they were regarded as 'at risk' at 7 years of age.

In the next chapter further test results on two groups of these
children will be discussed – an experimental group of those who
were most severely backward at 8 years of age, and another
group chosen from those who were less severely backward. The
case-histories of the 19 most severely backward readers at the age

of 9, as indicated in Table 16 (p. 80), will also be presented. Thanks to the assistance of their headmasters and co-operation of their parents, it was possible to supplement the test results with information on their pre-school and school development as seen by their families.

Chapter 8
Reading Difficulty, and What Else?

The Sample

The discussion in the preceding chapter was on the *reading level* at 9 years of age of all children who were 'at risk' at 7 years of age, and who were of average intelligence. All those with average intelligence and a reading score of 21 or less on the Southgate Reading Test were, however, given a wide range of tests in addition to the Neale Analysis of Reading Ability. The single criterion of a reading score of 21 or less meant a reading age of 7 years or less after 3 years at school, and would have included 120 children, or about half the group of backward readers. The intelligence level for inclusion was at least one IQ on WISC within the average range (i.e. full scale, verbal or performance IQ 90 or above). The double criterion of low reading level and average intelligence was met by 70 children (47 boys and 23 girls). As one of the boys left the county at this stage, there were 69 children in the experimental group. Had a more stringent criterion for intelligence been used, not only would the total size of the group have been reduced, but also the proportion of girls, as may be seen in Table 17.

Another group was chosen from those who had also been at risk but had a Southgate score of 22 or more. This was selected in such a way that both boys and girls independently were of comparable intelligence to the boys and girls in the experimental group. A check was made to ensure that the control group did differ from the experimental group not only on the Southgate test at 8 years of age, but also on accuracy and comprehension as assessed by the Neale test at the age of 9. Briefly, the control group was selected so that it met the following criteria:

1. Similar to the other non-experimental children for Neale reading scores; but different from the experimental children.

Table 17 Levels of Intelligence of all Children with Reading Score 21 or Less on Southgate Test at 8 Years of Age

Intelligence on WISC	Frequencies		
	Boys	Girls	Total
All 3 IQs at least 100	7	2	9
Full IQ at least 100	9	5	14
Verbal IQ at least 100	11	4	15
Performance IQ at least 100	18	7	25
At least one IQ at least 100	22	9	31
All 3 IQs at least 90	28*	8	36*
Full IQ at least 90	37*	12	49*
Verbal IQ at least 90	33*	9	42*
Performance IQ at least 90	42*	22	64*
At least one IQ at least 90	47*	23	70* ⎫
			⎬ 120
Without any IQ at least 90	22	28	50 ⎭

*One boy indicated by asterisk in table (all 3 IQs at least 90) left before further testing. Thus third-stage sample was 69 (46 boys and 23 girls).

Notes:

These are not cumulative frequencies – thus all those with *All 3 IQs at least 100* are included in those with *All 3 IQs at least 90*. The last two lines of the table together include all those with Southgate score 21 or less.

The criteria used for the third-stage testing were Southgate score 21 or less *and* at least one IQ at least 90, which included 47 boys and 23 girls.

2. Similar in intelligence to the other non-experimental children; and as near as possible to the experimental children.*

3. Representative for each sex separately rather than for the sexes combined.†

*This was difficult to achieve, as there was a tendency for those who improved in reading to be of higher intelligence; yet this matching was essential to avoid a difference in intelligence being the factor causing any apparent test differences.

†Already the study had revealed sex differences not only in absolute numbers, but also in pattern of results for the two sexes.

Details of the extent to which these three criteria were met may be seen in Table G in the appendix. The size of this group was pragmatically determined, in that it was the largest number of children meeting the criteria which could be tested in the available time up until the summer vacation of 1968.

Test Details

The testing at this stage of the research required about half a day per child with the experimental group, to which the *Illinois Test of Psycholinguistic Abilities* (ITPA) was administered in addition to the other tests planned for the total group (McCarthy and Kirk, 1961). This test, which has been administered in the United States to groups of handicapped children, including children with reading difficulties, and has been used in Britain in a few studies, is claimed to provide diagnostic information on important areas of language development. It provides, in addition to a language age, separate assessments of the child's position on the 9 sub-tests which constitute the scale. The test, which is still in an experimental edition, has no British norms, and has a ceiling of 9 years 3 months. It seemed worthwhile to administer it to the experimental group – even though by this time they were very near to the ceiling – in the hope that deficiencies in certain of the sub-tests might be revealed in the most severely backward of the group. The time taken to test the control group was about one hour per child. One problem in this aspect of the study was the need to prevent fatigue, and to ensure the continued co-operation of the child. The order of presentation of the tests was carefully planned with this in mind, ensuring that easy and more difficult tests were alternated, and that those involving reading were as widely separated as possible. Inevitably, the successful administration of the battery owed a great deal not only to the planning of the testing programme but also to the skill and sensitivity of the testers. No child refused any part of the testing, and in most instances the children would willingly have returned for more.

In Table 18 details are given of the tests used, the order in which they were administered, and the source from which they were derived. This table is sufficiently detailed to reveal the areas covered, and to set the scene for a discussion of the results. A number of tests were standard tests, others were modified for this study.

Table 18   Details of Testing for Stage 3

Order	Name of test and description	Type	Source
1	*Bender Gestalt Test* Copying a series of designs; Koppitz scoring of errors was used	V M	published test: Bender (1946), Koppitz (1964)
2	*Illinois Test of Psycholinguistic Abilities* Language test with 9 sub-tests on different aspects of language (experimental group only)	A V M	published test: McCarthy and Kirk (1961)
3	*Birch and Belmont Tapping Test* Ten tapped patterns, each to be matched from memory to one of 3 visual patterns	A V	from Birch and Belmont (1964)
4	*Wepman Test of Auditory Discrimination* Forty pairs of spoken words, some with a vowel or consonantal sound different; the child has to say whether they are the same or different	A	published test: Wepman (1958)
5	*Neale Analysis of Reading Ability* Graded passages read orally and scored for accuracy and comprehension	R	published test: Neale (1966)
6	*Visual-Auditory Learning Test* Five cards, each with a design and a nonsense name given orally. The child has 3 attempts to learn to associate the name with the design	A V	from Monroe (1932, pp. 199–200)

Order	Name of test and description	Type	Source
7	*Analysis and Synthesis of Words with Common Phonic Units* Sets of progressively harder regular words which the child has to read	R	adapted from Schonell and Schonell (1960, pp. 64–5)
8	*Test of Visual Discrimination and Orientation* Matching of a picture or design to one of several alternatives	V	from Daniels and Diack (1958, pp. 113–23)
9	*Identification of First and Last Letters in Words* Ten spoken words whose first letter the child has to identify from a choice of 5, and 10 words whose last letter the child has to identify	A V	adapted from Daniels and Diack (1958, pp. 125–9)
10	*Differentiation of Right and Left* Ten questions on ability to differentiate right and left on persons, and 3 objects in relation to one another	A	adapted from Zazzo and Galifret-Granjon (1964)
11	*Matchbox Test* Speed in changing matches from one box to another with right and with left hand (this was omitted from the analysis, as results varied with different testers)	M	adapted from Isle of Wight Survey – Rutter, Tizard and Whitmore (in press)
12	*Questions on Attitude to Reading* Knowledge of words and letters and amount of reading at home		

R = Reading
V = Visual
M = Motor
A = Auditory

All that is possible in the present report is a brief consideration of the more important results of these 111 children (69 severely backward and 42 less backward). Particular attention will be directed to the experimental group, and the results of the control group will be included in so far as they throw light on the problems of these children. The results of the boys and of the girls are given separately as it was clear throughout the study that sex differences were important, even when the intelligence and reading criteria for inclusion in the study were identical for the two sexes. The results of the 19 children who were most backward in reading at the age of 9 (all in the experimental group) will be discussed in more detail in the next chapter.

Reading

The groups considered here were selected on the basis of reading level at 8 years of age on a single test requiring the child to circle the appropriate word from a choice of 5. One year later, on a test of accuracy and comprehension when reading continuous prose, the experimental boys were markedly more backward than the control boys; for the girls the pattern was similar, with little overlap between the two groups. Looking back to the first test at the age of 7, which involved recognition of words out of context, it was also true that the experimental children had a lower reading quotient. Thus, selecting groups on the basis of one reading test, it was still possible to look back, or forward, to results on a different reading task and find a difference between the groups.

A diagnostic reading test, the Schonell Test of Analysis and Synthesis of Words Containing Common Phonic Units (Schonell and Schonell, 1960), was given to all these children at the age of 9. This test is used to assess the extent to which a child is able to deal with *regular* words in isolation. The words are arranged in order of difficulty from 'nip' to 'refreshment'. Normally the test is used only to check whether the child has acquired this skill. Here, however, testing was continued until the child failed 8 of 10 successive words. There was a marked difference in score on this test between the two groups:

Experimental boys: mean 31·4; standard deviation 19·6
Control boys: mean 76·8; standard deviation 11·7
Experimental girls: mean 41·1; standard deviation 22·6
Control girls: mean 73·8; standard deviation 12·2

Only 2 children in the control group scored less than 50, and none under 40.

Clearly, even at the age of 9, most of the experimental group had difficulty even with phonic analysis. Further confirmation of this was found in their responses when asked what they would do if they met a word they didn't know – 'ask the teacher', 'miss it out', 'shout for help' were some of the replies! Few suggested that they would sound it out. It didn't seem to occur to them that there was a pattern in many words which might assist in breaking the code. When asked to explain 'a letter' and 'a word', or failing that give examples, there was evidence of a vagueness concerning words and letters akin to that found by Jessie Reid in her study of 5-year-old children starting school (Reid, 1966). Even when tackling words which were regular, they often looked no further than the first letter before guessing. Yet many of them were struggling along in a large class, even in some instances with a book appropriate to their age rather than their ability.

A modification of one of the Daniels Reading Tests was also used (Daniels and Diack, 1958). The child has to listen to a word such as 'man' and select from 5 letters the one which represents the initial sound; this is followed by a series of words such as 'rub' whose final sound the child has to identify in the same way. This task gave greater difficulty to the experimental group, particularly when they were required to isolate the final sound.

Auditory Discrimination

In the Wepman *Auditory Discrimination Test* (Wepman, 1958) the child, with his back to the tester, has to indicate whether the same word has been said twice, or two different words. The words may differ either in consonant or vowel; for example, shake–shape or pat–pet. Thirty pairs are different, 10 are the same, these latter being used to ensure that the child has understood the task. Wepman states that children achieve the necessary powers of discrimination by the age of 8, and, since the words are pronounced loudly and clearly, only an occasional error is to be expected in children of 9 years of age. Error scores of 4 or more were made by over half these children, but error scores of 9 or more were confined to 8 children, all in the experimental group. Clearly there are a number of possible causes of poor auditory discrimination, not least of these being partial or high-frequency deafness. For that reason audiometric screening was arranged for all these children after the official completion of this study. A poor speech model at home might well have contributed to the lack of discrimination in some of the children; certainly hearing loss did not account for all of these children with poor auditory discrimination. What a study such as this cannot establish is whether poor auditory discrimination was a *cause* of their failure in reading, or whether success in reading might have helped the development of such discrimination. There is evidence from other studies that poor auditory discrimination may be causally related to poor school attainment (Durrell and Murphy, 1953; Wepman, 1960; Thompson, 1963; Christine and Christine, 1964). The deficiency in this area of so many of these children, combined with their failure in reading, may well mean that development of listening skills *for such children* may be a useful aspect of their remedial programme.

Visual Discrimination

The *Daniels Test of Visual Discrimination and Orientation* (Daniels and Diack, 1958) is a simple task of selecting from 5 alternatives the appropriate picture, design or word which matches the stimulus at the beginning of the line. It is not a memory task. A number of children in this study failed to make these gross discriminations even in pictures or designs (34 made more than 4 errors): it is thus not surprising that they failed to make the finer discrimination between words or between letters – particularly when short- or long-term memory is required, and not merely matching. Research in the field of visual perception does not give support to the idea that practice in visual matching tasks in general will transfer to discrimination on words (Vernon, 1957). The nearer the training is to the skill required, the more efficient the training is likely to be.

Motor Co-ordination

When asked to copy the designs of the *Bender Visual Motor Gestalt Test* (Bender, 1946), both the experimental and the control groups made higher error scores than would be expected from children of their age. The control group (boys mean 4·6, standard deviation 3; girls mean 4·5, standard deviation 2·9) was on the level expected of an 8-year-old, while that of the experimental group (boys mean 5·5, standard deviation 2·6; girls mean 5·7, standard deviation 2·6) was on the level expected of a 7-year-old. The Koppitz scoring system used here has been used in a number of studies on school progress (Koppitz, 1964). The type of errors she found to be significant with regard to school progress and which she therefore included in her scoring system are rotation of designs and incorrect placing of the parts in relation to each other, rather than gross motor co-ordination. Clearly a child who fails to appreciate, or is unable to reproduce, simple designs in their appropriate orientation (up to 45° error is permitted) and in their correct juxtaposition is not likely to appreciate the importance of the much finer discriminations of letters or even words. Studies have been made of the value of this test as a *predictor* of reading failure, both administered individually as in this present study, and also on group administration, either when each child has his own copy of the design or when a single large copy is displayed at the front of the room. Under each of these conditions the test was found to be a useful predictor of school progress (Smith and Keogh, 1962, 1963; see also Lachmann, 1960; Brenner *et al*, 1967; Koppitz, 1958a, 1958b, 1964). Some problems in the use of the Koppitz scoring have, however, been reported by Broadhurst and Phillips (1969).

It is important that teachers appreciate the significance of providing children who have difficulties in visuo-motor co-ordination with a model of letters and figures to which they can appeal if in doubt. If they have such difficulties, it seems pointless to expect them to rely on memory. They must see the correct visual pattern as often as possible, both on a model and in their own writing, rather than be frequently confronted with a variety of incorrect versions. Their attention requires to be drawn not only to differences in letters which *are* critical to letter discrimination, for example, orientation discriminating 'b', 'd' and 'p', but also to differences which are not critical to such discrimination, for example, size of letter and type of print.

Visual-Auditory Co-ordination

Two of the tests used in the study, that based on the Birch and Belmont studies and the *Monroe Visual Learning Task*, require the co-ordination of visual and auditory stimuli. In the *Tapping Test* (Birch and Belmont, 1964) a pattern of taps is presented to the child, who is asked to select the appropriate one of three visual patterns of dots which represents the same sequence; ten patterns are presented. The results were similar to those found by Birch and Belmont. The experiment group was particularly poor at this task (boys mean 4·6, girls 5·4; control group 7·3 and 6·2). A child may obtain a low score either because he has no strategy and just guesses, or because, though he has a strategy, he fails to remember the pattern long enough to translate it accurately into the visual pattern. Most children who failed here appeared to have no strategy. Their lack of a learning strategy was even more apparent in the Monroe Visual Learning Task (Monroe, 1932). Five cards are presented, each with a design on it, and a nonsense name is given orally. The child is shown each card in turn and asked to try and remember its name. The cards are then shown again *in the same order* and the child is asked to supply the names. This is done three times and the cards are always presented in the same order. Few of these children developed a strategy even by the third trial.

Ability to Discriminate Right and Left

These children were tested on their ability to discriminate right and left in themselves and in objects in relation to one another, on 10 items based on a translation from Zazzo and Galifret-

Granjon (1964), having previously been tested on a simpler task at 7 years of age. Even now that they were 9 years of age only 5 of the experimental and 7 of the control group made no errors; and these were among the better readers.

Laterality

The incidence figures for the various laterality characteristics of hand and eye for the total group were discussed on pages 45–9. Of the 69 children in the experimental group, 5 boys and 2 girls were left-hand writers, 3 boys and 1 girl used a different hand for writing and throwing, and the remainder were right-handed in both tasks. Left-eyedness was found in 16 boys and 10 girls, mixed-eyedness in 2 boys and 1 girl, and the remainder were right-eyed. The incidence of crossed laterality (hand and eye preference on opposite sides) varies according to the criterion used (see pp. 48–9). There was no evidence that it was any different in the experimental or control groups from that found in the total sample.

Illinois Test of Psycholinguistic Abilities (ITPA)

At the time of this study the ITPA, which is a test of various aspects of language development devised by J. J. McCarthy and S. A. Kirk in Illinois (1961), was still in an experimental edition. As there is no adaptation for British children, and as the children in this study were at the top end of the test since they were almost 9 years of age, it was used only on the experimental groups in order to ascertain whether they were below the expected level and whether any of the sub-tests were particularly discriminating. As the test takes almost one hour per child, it was not possible with the available staff to use it on the control groups – at least not before they were too old for the tables of norms. The mean language ages of the experimental boys and girls were well below their actual ages (boys mean 7 years; girls mean 6 years 10 months). Disappointingly little discrimination based on sub-test analysis was found (see Figure 10). A study by Mittler and Ward (1970) of 5-year-old twins using ITPA indicated that British children do score in line with the American norms, though Phillips (1968)

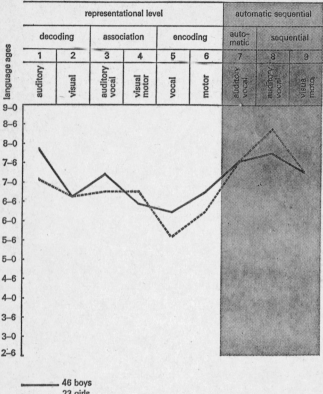

Figure 10 Mean Scores of Experimental Subjects on Sub-Tests of ITPA

cast doubts on some of the sub-tests. American studies have shown the ITPA to be a useful diagnostic measure in backward readers (Kass, 1963). Deficiencies in backward readers have been noted by some in tasks involving 'sequencing', which is required in ITPA auditory-vocal sequencing, memory for digits, and visual-motor sequencing, in which the child has to arrange a series of design cards in the same order as that shown previously by the tester. As can be seen from the profile, neither the boys nor the girls in this study *as a group* scored particularly low on these sequencing tests. There was still the possibility that certain individual children might have shown deficiencies in this area. Interesting remedial techniques based on tests such as these are described in *Reading and Remedial Reading* by Tansley (1967).

A number of weaknesses in the ITPA test were noted, some concerning its use with British children (such as the unfamiliarity with some of the pictures), others of more general concern, for example, the length of time required for the visual-motor sequencing test with a child who has an isolated success on a second trial, and the excess of musical instruments in the motor encoding test. The revised edition is greatly improved in many ways, and has a simpler terminology.

The discussion in this present chapter has been concerned with difficulties in groups of backward readers. In other studies patterns of impairment have been considered (Lovell and Gorton, 1968; Doehring, 1968). An analysis of the main patterns of impairment will be carried out on the present data. The need for an assessment of the difficulties of each individual child and for remedial work directed to assisting him is evident from the present study. An analysis of the results of the 19 most severely backward readers will underline the diversity of difficulties even in this single community. The findings here may alert teachers to possible areas of difficulty, and they should also draw attention to the fact that in a group of backward readers the disabilities are frequently not specific to the reading task, even when the children are all of average intelligence.

Chapter 9
Nineteen Severely Backward Readers

The children who were found to be most severely backward in reading at 9 years of age will be described in detail in this chapter. In addition to the 3 test sessions when these children were 7, 8 and 9 years of age, a parent of each of the children was interviewed when the child was about 10 years of age. Details were collected about size of family; birth history; pre-school development; illnesses of the child and of other members of the family; attitude to the school and to education.

The names of all 111 children (i.e. 69 experimental and 42 control children) in the final stage of the study were sent to the County Educational Psychologist, who was asked to state which children had been referred to the child guidance service, when, and for what reason. There was no indication on the list as to which were the 19 to be discussed here. Sixty of the children in the total group of 111 were referred to the child guidance service at some time before the age of 10 years. 'Backwardness' or 'assessment' were the stated cause of referral in 50 of the cases; possible mental handicap in 4; and only 3 were referred for 'behaviour difficulties', one as 'anxious' and one for 'speech difficulty'. Half the referrals were in 1966–7 after the children had been 2 years at school, and at the beginning of the research; there were approximately equal numbers before and after that date. Thirteen of this present group of children were referred, and the pattern of referral was similar to that for the rest of the group.

The head teachers in all the schools which contained any of the 111 children were asked to state whether each child was in the appropriate class for his age-group, what remedial help had been given, and for how long. Again, there was no indication on the lists as to whether the child was in the experimental or the control group. Forms were returned by all the schools, in many cases with additional comments by the teachers. This inquiry was for the above information, and also to obtain the children's addresses so that the parents could be contacted in connexion with the proposed vision and hearing testing of this complete group. Most of the children were taken to local clinics for vision testing. The parents of all 19 children in the severely backward group co-operated in this testing. As a consequence of the finding of poor auditory discrimination in a number of the children who were very backward, it was decided to test the hearing of the total group after the official end of the research. It was not possible to secure adequately sound-proofed testing conditions locally, so it was arranged that this testing take place on a Peters SPD5 audiometer in the sound-proof room at the University of Strathclyde. The children were transported by minibus in groups of 10 from all over Dunbartonshire. Again almost the entire group was included, except for one or two who had left the county, and a few absentees. Here again, all 19 were present. While the children were 'captive' in Strathclyde it was decided to make use of their waiting time to record on tape a sample of the speech of each child, on a modification of an articulation test at present being constructed in Edinburgh under the direction of Dr T. Ingram. It was therefore possible to analyse the speech of all 96 of these children who attended. They were also re-tested on the Schonell Graded Word Reading Test, used in the original screening when they were 7 years of age, and on the Daniels Spelling Test which had been given when they were 8. This time the test was administered from a tape recording, to provide a constant stimulus.

These investigations are the sources of the additional data referred to in this chapter. Brief comments on the results of the remainder of the group will be given in a later section.

In Table 19 the reading and spelling results of all 19 children, boys and girls, are shown, together with their intelligence level as assessed on the Wechsler Intelligence Scale when they were 8 years of age.* They are grouped in the table according to intelligence level, and the more detailed discussion is concentrated on the children who made higher scores on the intelligence test.

*The children's real names are not used.

Table 19 Intelligence, Reading and Spelling Levels of 19 Severely Backward Readers

Names	Intelligence WISC IQ			Reading					Spelling Daniels			Referred to child guidance*
	F	V	P	Schonell at 7+	at 10	Neale at 9 Acc	Neale at 10 Comp	Acc	Comp 8+	at 8+	at 10	
Boys												
David	101	100	105	5-5	7-10	7-0	6-9	7-11	7-6	7-1	8-1	Never
Alex	100	99	105	6-5	6-8	6-10	6-3	7-8	8-2	5-10	6-3	1968: backward
Roy	103	96	112	5-1	6-10	6-10	6-8	7-7	8-5	6-4	6-8	Never
Gordon	90	84	100	5-6	6-11	6-11	6-8	7-5	7-6	5-7	6-6	Never
Michael	94	94	98	5-1	7-8	NS	NS	7-11	8-5	5-4	7-5	1965: assessment
Donald	91	90	95	5-2	7-8	6-8	6-3	8-2	8-7	5-10	7-6	1967: backward
George	93	95	94	5-5	7-8	6-11	6-3	7-8	8-2	6-5	7-8	1966: assessment
Ian	94	99	92	5-2	6-6	6-5	6-3	7-2	7-10	5-2	6-4	1965: temper tantrums
Neil	92	96	91	NS	6-11	6-8	6-6	7-5	7-6	6-6	7-8	1965: assessment
Colin	85	90	84	5-1	7-8	6-6	6-11	7-9	8-5	5-5	7-0	1967: backward
Andrew	84	77	96	5-2	6-4	6-2	6-8	6-9	6-8	5-5	7-10	1966: assessment
Danny	90	86	98	NS	6-0	6-5	6-8	6-8	6-9	5-4	7-6	1967: assessment

	F	V	P									
Martin	91	87	98	NS	6-0	NS	6-6	NS	6-6	5-0	6-2	1966: backward
Jim	87	88	90	5-5	7-6	6-10	7-4	6-8	7-4	5-8	6-6	Never
Bobby	87	90	87	5-2	7-2	6-11	7-10	6-6	8-2	5-2	7-2	Never
Girls												
Catherine	91	84	92	5-5	7-2	6-10	7-11	6-6	8-2	5-7	7-4	Never
Margaret	81	78	90	NS	5-1	NS	NS	NS	NS	5-0	NS	1966: possibly MH
Helen	78	71	92	5-6	7-1	NS	7-8	NS	6-11	5-10	7-4	1965: possibly MH
Eileen	80	77	90	5-2	6-4	6-7	7-4	6-6	8-2	5-4	6-2	1966: by speech 1967: assessment

Intelligence: F = Full scale IQ; V = Verbal IQ; P = Performance IQ.
Reading: Acc = Accuracy; Comp = Comprehension; reading scores in years and months.
NS = No Score; MH = Mentally Handicapped.

*All these children started school in 1964.

Case 1. David, when first seen, could scarcely read a word. At the age of 9 his reading age on the Neale test was 7 years, which means that by then he just came into this group, and was in many other ways also the least backward. Already at 8 years of age when first tested on spelling he was making progress, with no evidence of reversals. His writing was legible; he had good auditory discrimination; and he was not confused visually or verbally in differentiation of right and left.

David had been in the same school throughout, with a low absence-rate. He was not regarded as a problem child by the school, as judged by the questionnaire completed by his teacher, and had never been referred to child guidance. His hearing and vision were normal, though according to his mother he had previously had a slight squint. On the speech test at the age of 10 there was no evidence of faulty articulation.

David is the last of five boys and is right-handed, as are all the family. Mother isn't sure how he is getting on at school, and feels he didn't get a great deal of attention when he was small as she was nursing 'Gran'. She reported nothing abnormal about his birth or development.

Here is a child who made a very slow start in reading and who, with remedial assistance in the school but little encouragement at home, has since then made slow but steady progress. When seen finally at the age of 10, David was in the class for his age-group, and had a reading and spelling age on about an 8-year level.

Case 2. Alex is a complete contrast to David. When first seen he already had a reading age of 6 years 5 months, and was by far the least backward of this group. On re-testing at the age of 9, however, his reading age was only 6 years 10 months. At 8, he could spell only 7 of the words on the Daniels test, but made no reversals. He was right-handed, and had adequate motor co-ordination. When seen at 9, he still had no idea how to sound out words, still only being able to look and guess. He scored low on most of the sub-tests of I T P A (language tests), and also showed very poor auditory discrimination.

Alex had few absences from school, but had changed school

after 2 years, and was in the class for his age. He had a high neurotic score on the questionnaire completed by his teacher, and this was confirmed by his mother, who mentioned among other things that he was shy and withdrawn. He had received no remedial help at school until recently, and was referred to the child guidance service only in 1968, because of backwardness.

Alex had two elder sisters aged 21 and 19, both right-handed. His mother reported that his speech development had been a bit slow, that he had got what he wanted by pointing. According to his mother, and confirmed by testing, he still confused 'f' and 'th'. There was no evidence of hearing defect.

At the time when he was last seen Alex had begun to show some improvement, with a Neale reading age of 7 years 8 months. He still could not tackle words in isolation, and was still only able to spell phonetically regular words. Here was a boy who had been only moderately backward, with a history of delayed speech and poor auditory discrimination, but who unfortunately suffered a change of school at the age of 7, to a school which was not able to provide the remedial assistance he required.

Case 3. Roy was another virtual non-reader at the age of 7, with few absences and no changes of school. He has made only slight progress with reading until recently, when some remedial assistance has been provided in the school. Previously he had for a time been sent privately, by his parents, for some assistance because of his speech defect associated with the reading difficulty. His faulty articulation was still evident at the age of 10, but there was no hearing defect.

Roy was hospitalized because of his own illness, and in a nursery because of his mother's tuberculosis, during his first 2 years of life. His mother feels that both he and his older brother are below average, though Roy is lower. His motor development was slow and he was clumsy. He was late in speaking, and ran his words together when he did start to speak. Both he and his brother are right-handed.

Case 4. Gordon had made only a slight start in reading at the age of 7. Like Roy he had good attendance and no changes of school, though the school he attended had suffered staff shortage, and Gordon had at one time different teachers in the morning and afternoon. His difficulty was in these circumstances less noticed than it would have been otherwise. He had a high anti-social score on the questionnaire completed by his teacher, but had never been referred to child guidance. His writing was illegible at the age of 8, and there were a few reversals in his later spelling attempt at the age of 10. His auditory discrimination was adequate, and his error score on the Bender test of motor co-ordination was low. His hearing and speech were normal.

Gordon is the second oldest of five children, his mother having previously lost three. She would like him to get on in school and would help him, but hasn't time. None of the children seems fit, though Gordon's developmental milestones were normal. She described him as not a good eater, bites his nails, frightened of noises, active, always on the go. She commented that it is difficult to get him to concentrate. This picture is similar to that found in school, where he appeared alert but restless, and where other children helped him to cover up his deficiencies in reading. It should be noted that his verbal intelligence was much lower than his score on the performance side, and his score on EPVT at the age of 7 was 79, which is also well below average, and would place him on a lower level verbally than his full scale IQ would indicate.

These four children have been described in some detail because they were still severely backward at the age of 9 years, and yet well within the average range for intelligence. As can be seen, in none of these cases was there any evidence of striking factors, either causative or associated with the disability, which had proved resistent to intensive remedial tuition. The next five children in the group had all IQs 90 or more, that is, within the normal range. *Michael* and *Donald* were in the same school and were both referred early to child guidance for assessment, one in 1965, the other in 1967. Again, from a poor initial start they had both made progress. Michael, who was much later in starting, had a very poor attendance record during his first 3 years at school.

Both were right-handed, and while Michael's auditory discrimination was poor, Donald had a high error score on the Bender test of motor co-ordination. Both were from small families; Michael was the younger of two, Donald the eldest of three. Nothing abnormal was mentioned in the development of either, except for a slight speech defect which Donald has. They were both described as good mixers. Neither was in the class for his age-group; and each had been in a tutorial class for a year with other children who were backward.

Case 7. George was youngest of five, had a speech defect at one time, which was mentioned both by his teacher and by his mother. He had both poor auditory discrimination and poor visuo-motor co-ordination as shown by the Bender test. He had attended school regularly and been in the same school throughout, where he had received remedial assistance over a period of years. His school had referred him to the child guidance service in 1966, with a request for assessment.

The remaining two children who had all three IQs within the normal range were both left-handed, the only two left-handed boys in the 15.

Case 8. Ian was referred to child guidance because of temper tantrums shortly after starting school, the only one to be referred for something unrelated to assessment. He got a very high score for anti-social behaviour on the questionnaire at the age of 8, and was still at the age of 10 described by the school as difficult. His mother independently described him as very restless, nervous, a poor sleeper, staying out late, and unable to keep friends. Ian is the fifth of eight children, three others of whom are left-handed. Mother had high blood pressure, and the birth was induced at the eighth month of pregnancy. The baby was blue at birth. He was separated from his mother from the age of 5 to 11 months, and was placed in a home as she was in hospital. Though not slow in speech development his speech was described as jumbled, and he had a stammer when excited. One of his brothers was a deaf, dumb and blind spastic in an institution. Deafness was suspected in Ian when he was 5, and he had running ears on a number of occasions; also, something lodged in his ear. There was still evidence of residual deafness in his right ear when he was tested at the age of 10 as part of this study, though his articulation was not markedly defective. His auditory discrimination was very poor; on the Wepman test at the age of 9 he made 12 errors out of 30 items. His writing was illegible when first seen at 8, while his visuo-motor co-ordination was also poor. At the age of 10 he had some reversals in his spelling, but was reading at the 7-year level on a continuous passage, though words in isolation and spelling gave him difficulty. His language scores on ITPA were low (four below 6 years, and two below 5 years), as was his score on EPVT, which was 79.

Ian had been at the same school throughout, and was seldom absent. Though in the appropriate class for his age, he has some remedial help.

Clearly Ian's problems, which go well beyond the area of reading, cannot be attributed to the reading failure, though it may have aggravated them. His mother and his teachers independently painted a picture of a restless, over-active, difficult child from his earliest years. Fluctuating deafness, poor motor co-ordination and a speech defect have all added to his difficulties. In spite of all this, he is at last making some progress with reading, if only limited success with spelling.

Case 9. Neil was last in a family of seven, one of his sisters also being left-handed. His mother described him as 'normal', but he was observed to bite his nails and fidget repeatedly during the test sessions. His motor development was slow as a result of an operation at 7 months for a double rupture, which prevented him from being allowed on his feet. The rupture was claimed to be the result of a difficult birth (a breech birth delivered by father). His mother felt that his speech was normal except for a slight difficulty in saying 'l'. His teacher, however, noted a speech defect and stammer, while on the speech test at 10 he was also found to have faulty articulation. A slight hearing loss in his left ear at some frequencies was also noted. In contrast with Ian his auditory discrimination was, however, adequate, as was his motor co-ordination. His writing was legible, and he made no reversals at the age of 10, with a low error score on the Bender test. Neil had failed to start reading at the age of 7, but by the age of 10 had attained reading and spelling ages of about 7 years 6 months. His whole school career had been in the same school, which had referred him for assessment in 1965, which was, as in the case of Ian, soon after he started school. Remedial assistance from the infants' mistress had been given from early in his school career. Neil was thought by his mother to require glasses, which was confirmed on our testing.

The remaining 6 boys had at least one I Q just over 90, but the highest full scale I Q was 91. There were many interesting points in their histories, but it is not possible to deal with them individually. The first four of this group in Table 19 (pp. 98-9) were referred early to child guidance for assessment. All these four were noted in the questionnaire at the age of 8 as having a speech defect; two of them, Colin and Martin, still had faulty articulation at the age of 10; three of them had a slight hearing loss on the audiometric testing; while the fourth, Colin, passed our test, but had recently failed with both ears in a test for which his teacher had referred him. Three of them had a very high absence-rate, Martin being absent half the first year, then quarter of each subsequent year; while Danny and Jim averaged a quarter of each school year in absence. These three were all from large families, Martin being one of seven, the others each one of five. Four of them had illegible writing at the age of 8, while Danny had a number of reversals then. None of them still made reversals at the age of 10. All but Bobby made a high error on the Bender test, showing inability to copy designs in the appropriate orientation even at the age of 9. In short, this represents the rather dull group of children who, if all other circumstances are favourable, may reach a minimum level of literacy by the middle of the primary school, but, with associated handicaps such as speech defect, hearing impairment, or even a very high absence-rate, may fall into the 'at risk' category. None of them, however, fits the classical description of a child suffering from specific reading disability.

Finally, what of the girls in this severely backward group? Using the same criterion for selection for each sex, there are only 4 girls in this group (see Table 19, pp. 98-9). Further, none of these girls would have been in the sample had the intelligence criterion for selection been more rigorous. Each had a performance IQ which just reached 90, but only in one instance was the verbal IQ even over 80. Only Margaret of these four was left-handed, but all four had poor auditory discrimination combined with poor visuo-motor ability as measured by the Bender test, and poor co-ordination as measured by their writing. All were good attenders and had been at only one school throughout, except for Catherine, who had changed out of and back into the same school for administrative reasons. She was the only one who had not early been referred to child guidance, as possibly mentally handicapped.

Case 1. Catherine had only one brother, older than herself. Her speech was described as slow, and this was attributed by her mother to her brother, who understood what she wanted. Apart from ear trouble between the ages of 3 and 4, her development was described by her mother as normal. She had made some progress both in reading and spelling by the time she was last seen at the age of 10. She was in the same school as one of the other girls, Margaret.

Case 2. Margaret's mother was resentful of the school and attempts which had been made to send Margaret to a special school; she was therefore unwilling to admit that there was anything abnormal in Margaret's development. An older sister was mentally handicapped and in an occupation centre, while a brother was difficult at school. The school says that the children are neglected, but the mother says she encourages independence. There was no evidence of a speech defect when Margaret was tested. On the occasion of our audiometric testing, however, she had a hearing loss with both ears on a wide range of frequencies. Suspected deafness was not mentioned by her mother. Her auditory discrimination at the age of 9 was not as poor as would have been expected from her level of hearing loss at the age of 10;

possibly her loss is a fluctuating one. Her mother had shown the initiative to take her privately for assessment in order to prevent her being sent to a special school. Margaret was still in her ordinary school at the age of 10, in the class for her age, and the only child seen at that age who was neither able to read nor write.

Case 3. Helen was the youngest in a family of nine and was said to be still tied to her mother and to 'put on crying' to get her own way. All the family were said to be a bit slow; one sibling was in an occupation centre and another in a special school, while her mother's sister could neither read nor write. Helen's speech was described by her father as normal, but by the teacher as defective. Her articulation was still found to be markedly faulty at the age of 10. She confused half the items on the test of auditory discrimination, but this did not appear to be associated with defective hearing. Helen's defective speech and her reading difficulty, coupled with her low intelligence, do not set her apart from the rest of her family.

Case 4. Eileen, the last child in this group, was perhaps the most tragic case in the sample. She was the only girl in a family of five. Three years ago her oldest brother died after a long illness, at which time Eileen's hair is reported to have fallen out. Mother describes herself and also the father as nervous. One of the boys is described as bright, but the others are slow, nervous and bed-wetters. Eileen's speech development was very slow and she had speech therapy over a period of years. Her articulation was still faulty when she was seen at the age of 10. Clearly, apart from her limited intelligence and defective speech, Eileen comes from a nervous, disturbed family, whose most severe crises came just at the time when she was learning to read. With a great deal of help since her first year at school she has made a certain amount of progress.

In describing these cases a great deal of selection from all the available data has been necessary. Bias has been inevitable in what has been included and what left out. Certain features were found to be striking in this group in contrast with even the remainder of the experimental group. One particularly marked characteristic was the occurrence of a speech defect of some kind. In no instance did the mother mention a defect which had not also been observed by the teacher. In 10 children with a reading age on the Neale test of 7 years or less at the age of 9, the teacher had noted a speech defect when completing the questionnaire. In a number of cases the defective articulation was still evident at 10 years of age. Of the 96 children whose speech was assessed at that age, only 7 boys and 3 girls were regarded as having markedly defective articulation; 4 of the boys were in this group of 15, and 2 of the girls were in this group of 4.

Poor auditory discrimination was another marked characteristic of the group. Twelve of the 19 had a high error score on the Wepman test; while 9 had a high error score on the Bender test, indicating that they had difficulty in copying simple designs with any degree of accuracy long after most children had mastered that skill. Ten of these children had writing at the age of 8 which was illegible, and therefore any tendency to reversals could not be analysed (4 who were legible made reversals at that age). There was little evidence of change of school within the group, but 4 had a consistently high absence-level. Left-handedness was found in 3 of the children (2 boys and 1 girl). Eight of the children, still at the age of 9, confused right and left either on themselves or on someone opposite them; interestingly enough, none of these 8 was left-handed. A number of these children came from large families, and generally speaking, though the attitude of the parents to education was favourable as revealed by the parental interview, there was little evidence of active assistance from the home. Few of these children mentioned being read to at home; unlike another child in the 'at risk' group, who commented that his mother used to read to him, but no longer did so now that he could read for himself. Reading within this group tended to be confined to 'my school reading book', or 'my sister's school reading book'.

A strikingly different pattern was found for the two sexes, not only in actual numbers of girls but also in the level of intelligence of the girls who were severely backward. In the hope of throwing some light on this, a separate analysis was made of pairs of children matched for intelligence and in the same school, all, at risk, at 7 years of age, but one of the pair a boy, the other a girl. These sex differences in reading will be considered in the next chapter.

Chapter 10
Sex and Reading

Among the group of 230 backward readers were boys and girls of similar intelligence yet very different reading levels, even within a single school. It was thought that a consideration of such children, matched for as many other variables as possible, but different in sex, might help to throw some light on the question of sex as an important variable predictive of reading failure. It had been noted earlier that the group of backward girls was not only smaller, but also of lower intelligence than the group of backward boys. Here, in spite of similar intelligence, both verbal and performance, were girls all making better progress than boys, in whichever school they happened to be.

It was found possible within the group of backward readers (138 boys and 92 girls) to select 8 *boy/girl pairs*; each pair matched rigorously for intelligence; both members of a pair in the same school; but each pair in a different school. In each pair both children were in the 'at risk' group at 7+, but in each case the girl was no longer in that group, whereas the boy with the same level of intelligence *and* in the same school still remained 'at risk'. No criterion with regard to intelligence was set for this group, as one interesting finding was the fact that such pairs were to be found at a wide range of intelligence levels, one even being in a special school. Most of this group were already in the main study either as experimental (boys) or control (girls). All 16 children were tested on the complete third-stage battery, including the Illinois Test of Psycholinguistic Abilities, and all were tested by the same psychologist. Details of the intelligence and reading levels in this group are shown in Table 20.

An attempt was made to find other types of paired groups for special study; for example boy/boy or girl/girl pairs differing in reading level but matched for intelligence; or girl/boy pairs where the boy had improved more than the girl. It was impossible to form such groups from this sample. Such pairs could be found

Table 20 Distribution of Reading and Intelligence in Group for Paired Comparison (8 Boy/Girl Pairs)

No. of pair	Sex	Southgate	Reading ages Neale Acc	Comp	Full	WISC IQ Verbal	Perform-ance
1	Boy	6:0	NS	NS	94	94	98
	Girl	7:6	9:6	7:3	94	94	98
2	Boy	6:8	7:2	8:2	94	96	95
	Girl	7:9	9:1	8:7	90	96	87
3	Boy	6:7	NS	NS	91	87	98
	Girl	7:5	7:7	7:6	91	87	98
4	Boy	6:6	6:3	6:8	90	86	98
	Girl	7:6	7:6	7:3	93	90	100
5	Boy	6:8	6:11	6:8	90	84	100
	Girl	7:3	7:10	7:6	89	83	99
6	Boy	6:7	7:5	6:8	87	84	94
	Girl	7:5	7:11	6:8	81	75	92
7	Boy	6:7	7:4	7:7	81	74	94
	Girl	7:3	8:7	6:1	77	68	94
8	Boy	5:9	NS	NS	66	72	64
	Girl	7:1	6:9	6:6	61	71	57

Southgate test and WISC at 8 years of age.

Neale Reading Test at 9 years of age.

NS = No Score. Acc. = Accuracy; Comp. = Comprehension.

less well-matched for intelligence, but it seemed important to match both for verbal and performance levels. Some pairs could have been found had the insistence on the pair being within the same school been abandoned. Here again, it seemed important to rule out the effect of type of school. Clearly, if 8 such pairs could be found within a group of 230 children, each pair in a different school, it does suggest that such a situation may be common within our educational scene.

In each of these 8 pairs both the boy and the girl started school at the same time in a mixed school, in most cases the same school, and there could be no more than 5 months difference in their ages. The complete test results are available for all these children. Two children were lost to the sample shortly after the testing was completed; the girl in Pair 2 who died, and the boy in Pair 6 who had been fostered within the county, and was removed to another county. For this reason parental interviews were not arranged, but the remaining 14 children did attend for audiometric testing and the follow-up at the age of 10. Four of the boys in this group were among the 19 discussed in the previous chapter; one other, though equally low in reading, was too dull to have been included; while the remaining 3 had reading ages on the Neale test above 7 years at the age of 9.

Pair 1. Both *Michael* and *Alison* were virtual non-readers when first seen, though of average intelligence. Both attended the same school throughout, where Michael was for some time in a tutorial class. Alison's attendance, unlike that of Michael, was good throughout, and, again unlike him, she was never referred to a psychologist. Their scores on EPVT at 7 years of age were similar. By the age of 8 Alison, in contrast with Michael, had made marked progress with both reading and spelling, with 26 words correct on the Daniels Spelling Test. Both were right-handed, and it was Alison who had the high error score on the Bender test; while they had comparable levels of auditory discrimination, Alison's language age on the ITPA was slightly higher, though the pattern of scores was very similar. By the age of 10 Alison scored a reading and spelling age of 10 years 2 months, whereas Michael, though making some progress, was only at the 7 years 8 months level. Alison's arithmetic was similarly in advance of Michael's. Both children were found to have a slight hearing loss when tested, but Michael's was over a wider range of frequencies, though only in one ear.

Pair 2. Stephen and *Mary* were also both of average intelligence. Mary moved into the county only shortly before the research started, because of her mother's death, and came to attend the same school as Stephen. He was the more severely backward when first seen, but Mary's EPVT score was much lower (76,104); his absence-rate was, however, high throughout. At the age of 8 Mary could already spell 23 words on the Daniels test, whereas Stephen was a non-speller; and by the age of 9 Mary scored a reading age for accuracy on the Neale test of 9 years 1 month, though her level of comprehension was similar to his. Mary died tragically during the summer of 1968. When Stephen was re-tested he had continued to make progress.

Pair 3. Martin and *Betty* (IQ 91) attended the same school. At the age of 9 Martin was still unable to read, while Betty was making progress with both reading and spelling. Surprisingly, on EPVT at 7 years of age Betty scored 60 and Martin scored 101. Both were referred to the psychologist as backward while still in the infant department. Their auditory discrimination was similar as were most of their other scores, with the exception of the ITPA (Martin's language age was 8 years 4 months and Betty's 6 years 10 months). Both had a slight hearing loss, though Betty's was only in one ear. Martin, in addition, had very defective articulation. By the age of 10 Betty's reading age on Schonell was 7 years 5 months, and her spelling level was similar; while Martin managed only 10 words on the Schonell test.

Pair 4. Danny and *Jean* were also still within the average range of intelligence, yet had made little progress at 7 years of age, both being referred to the psychologist for assessment. Even by 9 years of age Danny had made little progress, but his absence-rate was high throughout. By the age of 10 Jean scored 8 years 5 months on the Schonell test, on which Danny, like Martin, read only 10 words. Danny was making similar progress to Jean in spelling. Here again test results were similar for the two children, except for the ITPA, where Danny's language age was a year lower than Jean's. Both children had one change of school during the study.

Pair 5. Gordon and *Susan* spent their first few years in the same school and were similarly poor in reading when first seen. On the performance side they scored within the average range, but were both much lower on the verbal side. Susan's EPVT score was higher than Gordon's, as was her language age on the ITPA. Her attendance was poor throughout, whereas Gordon was rarely absent. Yet Susan began to make progress and continued to hold her lead over Gordon. By 8 she could spell and he could not; by the age of 10 she was still over a year ahead in reading, and 2 years ahead in spelling. Susan had been referred for assessment in 1966, but Gordon was never referred. The remaining test scores were similar.

Pair 6. This pair were of lower intelligence than those discussed previously. *Tom* was referred in 1966 as possibly mentally handicapped, and *Ann* in 1967. Though the level of intelligence of these two children was very similar, their histories were very different. Both started in the same school. Tom, a foster child, was transferred to a special school and ultimately left the county. Ann, of similar level of intelligence on our testing but with a slightly higher level of attainments, remained in her ordinary school. Ann was left-handed, the only one in this group; apart from that these children had similar results on the test batteries. No further information is available on Tom. No deficiencies were observed in Ann when she was seen at 10 years of age, and she was by then reading and spelling on an 8-year level.

Pair 7. Peter and *Sheila* were of low intelligence with a marked discrepancy between verbal and performance scores on WISC, and were almost non-readers at the age of 7. Both also had low scores of 76 on EPVT on first testing, and both were right-handed. They remained in the same large school throughout, where Sheila's attendance was slightly poorer during the first 2 years. When tested at 8 years of age Sheila's reading was much better than Peter's, and her spelling slightly better. Both were referred early to the child guidance service; Sheila was referred in 1965 as very withdrawn, while Peter was referred a year later as backward. Peter spent some time in a tutorial class and his teacher there wondered whether he was deaf, but no confirmation of this was found. Our psychologist also questioned his hearing when he was 9, but again on our audiometric testing at 10 he was clear. Sheila, on the contrary, was found on our testing at 10 to be severely deaf. Without the aid of lip-reading she was unable to repeat numbers correctly. This would appear to be transitory, though worth checking. She certainly was suffering from catarrh on that occasion. Her error level on the Wepman Test of Auditory Discrimination when she was 9 was similar to Peter's and not as high as would have been expected from the hearing loss exhibited on this later occasion. Also, her speech was without any articulatory defects, while Peter's was noted as defective. At the age of 9 Peter had a reading age on the Neale test of 7 years 4 months, not one of the most severely backward, while Sheila was a year ahead on accuracy though poor on comprehension. At the age of 10 Sheila had retained her lead (Schonell reading age 9 years 4 months against Peter's 7 years 6 months). Both were now able to spell on a 7-year level. Sheila's spelling was much better than this score would indicate. Her hearing was so badly affected on that occasion that she frequently spelt the wrong words, though they were correctly spelt. The words were given in a sentence, but from a tape recorder, so that she had no visual cue. All the third-stage results on these two were comparable, whether ITPA, Bender where they both had a low error score, or ability to differentiate right and left, where they were both confused. Even their scores on the adjustment questionnaire were similar. No explanation for the difference in their attainment was to be found in the test results.

Pair 8. Stuart and *Claire* were of very low intelligence, both verbal and performance, and were therefore not in the final phase of the main study. Stuart was referred to child guidance in 1965 as very backward, while Claire was referred in 1966 as backward and because of the family situation. They were not at the same school originally, but were both early referred to the same special school, where Claire made some progress with both reading and spelling, while Stuart made none; yet her language age on the ITPA (5 years 6 months at 9 years of age) and most of her other test scores were similar to Stuart's. Both had high error scores on the Bender test of visuo-motor co-ordination. Stuart's auditory discrimination was, however, very poor and also his articulation as assessed on the speech test, though neither child was found to have any hearing impairment. Claire looked alert and enthusiastic, and had a deceptive air of brightness, an impression which was immediately dispelled when she was set any task involving intelligence; though willing, she was certainly not able. With an IQ of 61 Claire had a reading age on Schonell of 6 years 6 months, and a spelling age on the Daniels test of 7 years 1 month at the age of 10 years; while Stuart could neither read nor write.

The purpose of this aspect of the study was not a statistical analysis of any general discrepancies between the groups of boys and girls. This could more appropriately be analysed in the main study. What was of concern was to determine whether there were any consistent differences associated with reading level between the members of the pairs. The only justifiable conclusion from a study of the results of these 8 pairs of children is that when the level of intelligence is as carefully and closely matched as it was in these children, the test results do not explain the difference in reading and spelling level. In some pairs the boy was better in a test, in others the girl. The only place where differences were consistently in favour of the girls were in the aspects directly related to reading. This section is presented as a warning against too ready acceptance of superficially adequate explanations of differences in level of attainment in reading and spelling. All the girls were making progress in both reading and spelling, whatever their level of intelligence, while the boys, matched for intelligence, length and type of schooling, were making slow or little progress. Are there other aspects of intellectual development which were not assessed here which are crucial variables? *Or* are there other aspects of development which were not assessed and which are more important – for example, motivation and concentration? Persistence when faced with difficult words certainly seemed more apparent in the girls, who tended to be willing to continue struggling with the words they didn't know, by contrast with the boys. However, this observation may be selective perception or examiner bias, as the tester was a woman! *Or* is the difference one of perception of the learning situation by the two sexes? The attitude of a boy and a girl to severe failure may be different even when of the same level of intelligence. *Or* is it a question of attitude to school and teachers? Would there be any marked effect on the level of backwardness in boys if more men taught reading, or if reading books were different and more geared to the interests of boys?

Clearly there is no simple or single answer. There are comparative studies in different countries of incidence levels of backwardness, and in all these studies boys predominate. Need they predominate by so much? 'Delayed maturation' is the expression which is usually advanced as the explanation for the excess of vulnerable boys. It is not being suggested that this is no explanation, but the girls in this study were still ahead at 10 years of age. Is delayed maturation the complete explanation?

Chapter 11
One Year Later

Arrangements were made for as many as possible of the children in the third-stage sample, experimental and control, to attend the University of Strathclyde during two weeks in April 1969 for audiometric testing. Considering the history of absence of some of these children, it is astonishing how few of them missed this visit. Of all who had been in the sample one year previously, 96 attended on this occasion, 6 had left the county, one had died, and 8 were absent. Of the absentees, 3 were from the experimental group and 5 from the control group. Only 3 of the 8 had a reading age under 8 years on the Neale test at the age of 9 (7 years 4 months being the lowest). Arrangements were also made to test the vision of these children in local clinics, and to this the children were taken by their parents. Here also there was a surprisingly low absence-rate. Eight children failed to attend for vision testing (3 of these were also missing from the audiometric testing). Only 4 of these had reading ages under 8 years. None of the most severely backward readers were missing on either of these occasions; nor were any of the remaining 14 children in the boy/girl pairs. Claire and Stuart, Pair 8 in the study, and the only pair not in the main study, also attended, and their results have been discussed in the preceding chapter. They will not, however, be included here, as they did not meet the intelligence criterion. The results of the audiometric survey and the ophthalmic study for the whole sample will also not be considered in detail here, but will be reported elsewhere. Any relevant findings on the children in the special studies were mentioned in their case-histories in the two preceding chapters. Two points only will be made at the present stage. It is interesting to note in connexion with the vision of this group that corrected vision was recorded for about one-third of these children in the ophthalmic report – yet when attending Strathclyde for the audiometric survey, hardly any of these children were wearing glasses. Unfortunately the results of the vision testing became available only after the commencement of the other testing, or a note would have been made of the actual children who were wearing glasses on that occasion. If corrected, the vision may well be adequate, but we have no record as to how long it was before the correction was prescribed, nor on how many occasions! This is a common finding with glasses; that it is one thing to prescribe them, another to ensure that they are worn and clean. General analysis of hearing loss within the group did not indicate marked differences in reading level between those children who had slight hearing loss and those who had not, nor between those who had a loss within the speech frequencies and those who had a loss outside these frequencies. There were, nevertheless, examples of individual children in whom it appeared that hearing loss might have been a contributory factor.

In several children hearing loss at certain frequencies combined with faulty articulation. The results of the most severely backward children on the articulation test were mentioned earlier. This test necessitated only that the child respond with one word either to the stimulus of a picture in the first 20 items, or an object in the other 20 items. The child's responses were recorded on tape and analysed later. In fact, apart from the locally accepted variant of 'chimley' for 'chimney', there were few children with faulty articulation by 10 years of age. One or two still substituted 'f' for 'th'. Most of those whose faults were more general were among those with the lowest reading levels (see pp. 73). Early speech difficulties have been found, by Ingram, Mason and Blackburn (1970) and De Hirsch, Jansky and Langford (1966) for example to be associated in a number of cases with later reading difficulties.

The Schonell Graded Word Reading Test, on which these children had been tested 3 years before as part of the full sample of 1544, was repeated on this occasion. The Daniels Spelling Test, on which they had been tested 2 years before as part of the sample of 230 backward readers, was also repeated. It was presented on tape on this occasion to provide a constant stimulus, because of the variations in mis-spellings noted on the previous occasion as a result of different people administering the test. It is perhaps a fitting conclusion to the study to present the results of these children who stayed the course from 1966 until 1969, and who did not manage to escape from the county. It is possible from the results on this occasion to determine how many of these children were still severely backward, either in reading or spelling, after 5 years at school (see Table 21).

Table 21 Reading and Spelling Level of Backward Readers at 10 Years of Age

	No. of children at each level				
	7 yrs or less	7·1– 8 yrs	8·1– 9 yrs	9·1 or more	Total
Reading on Schonell test	12	37	27	20	
					96
Spelling on Daniels test	19	31	29	17	

Thus half of this group were still 2 or more years backward on this test of accuracy of reading words in isolation, while 12 of them were 3 or more years backward, that is, were still unlikely to be able to use reading as a means of securing information or enjoyment. Ten of these 12 children were among the 19 discussed earlier, the remainder of that group having scores ranging from 7 years 1 month to 7 years 10 months. The remaining 2 boys, both from the same school, had just escaped the severe group on the Neale test at the age of 9 (with reading ages of 7 years 1 month and 7 years 2 months), but seemed to have made little progress since. The spelling of these two was on a similar level, one making a number of reversal errors.

There was a marked tendency for the children in this group who were able to read also to be able to spell. Only 7 of the children whose reading level was above the 7-year level were spelling below that level. Of those with reading ages above the 8-year level, 12 had spelling ages below 8 and only one had a spelling age below 7 years. At least the minimum essentials of spelling had been acquired by most of these children. Reversals were again analysed to determine how common they remained at this stage. The greatest number of reversals in a single child was 7; these were instances, not types of reversal. Two children had 4 reversals, two had 3; five had 2, and six had 1, which was either 'b' for 'd' or 'd' for 'b'. There were also a few children who still had inversion errors, such as 'p' for 'b', and a few who reversed the letter order, for example, 'aer' for 'are'. Reversal of letters was not found specifically associated with left-handedness, but as a common error in those children who had a low spelling level.

Part Four
Summary and Implications

Chapter 12
Summary and Implications

All children in the County of Dunbartonshire who were born between 1 April and 31 August 1959 were tested after they had completed 2 years at school, and were just over 7 years of age. The most important results from the community study of 1544 children were as follows:

1. About 15 per cent of the children in this county were without any independent reading skill in 1966, after they had been 2 years at school.

2. Boys were found to be backward in a slightly greater proportion than girls, and to be more likely to continue to have difficulty.

3. Many children still confused left and right in themselves or other people at 7 years of age – whether or not they were backward in reading. Only one quarter of the children were without any such confusion even on 5 simple items.

4. The motor co-ordination required to copy a diamond to an acceptable standard was shown by only 31·8 per cent of the children at the age of 7, which would mean that many children could be expected to find difficulty in reproducing all the letters of the alphabet in a distinguishable form. When this is taken in conjunction with the preceding statement, the occurrence of reversals of letters and reversed letter order in words should not be a matter for surprise, particularly when a child has not a model of the letter available for comparison.

5. There was no evidence that left-handedness, left-eyedness or any combination of these was predictive of reading level in this population.

6. Absence-rate in the total group was high in the first year, and though slightly lower in the second year was found to be associated with reading level. Not only total absence but also pattern

of absences would be of importance, but this was not analysed in this study.

7. Changes of school were a common occurrence, not only within the county but also from outside the county. One child in 4 had been in at least 2 schools in the first 2 years. In view of the finding of both high absence-rate and high mobility-rate it seems important that some written record be kept of a child's progress, the approach to reading, his difficulties, etc., and that some such information accompany the child who changes school. This seems particularly important in view of the additional factor of rapid turnover of staff, an aspect which was not specifically studied in this present investigation. The importance of the role of the infants' mistress and head teacher as co-ordinators of policy which were stressed by Dr Morris would seem to be crucial in the light of the kind of conditions found in this study.

The most severely backward readers in the county were tested again after they had completed 3 years at school, and the results on these 230 children were as follows:

1. Half of these children were still requiring assistance in the basic skill of reading even at that stage. Though this included all children in the county *whatever their level of intelligence*, it was not a problem which could be passed over in its entirety to the special schools. Some form of organization was required within the junior schools to assist the class teacher to deal with the problem. These children were by then at a stage when reading was a tool subject and written work would be required of them. It was unrealistic to expect the class teacher alone to deal with them, though it was felt to be important that she recognize them and that she be involved in their treatment, since they would remain in her classroom for the greater part of the day.

2. Most of those children who were improving in reading were also making some progress with spelling. A small proportion of this group had not yet grasped sound–symbol relationship well enough to write even simple regular words.

3. Reversals or inversions of letters, or reversed letter order in words, was found to be a common occurrence in children who were still learning the mechanics of reading. Almost half of these backward readers made some reversals, whatever their preferred hand. There was no evidence that the left-handed children were any more likely to make such faults than right-handed children of the same level of intelligence. Clearly a number of the backward readers had not yet learnt to *recognize* sound–symbol relationship, let alone to *reproduce* it as is required to spell correctly.

4. The girls who were backward readers formed a smaller and a duller group than the boys. A girl seemed to be in little danger of being severely backward in reading unless she was also dull. A further analysis of boy/girl pairs who were matched for intelligence indicated that this was a more complex issue than it appeared at first sight (see chapter 10).

5. There were children of average intelligence who were severely backward in reading at the age of 7, but the majority of such children were of low average intelligence.

6. When assessed separately on the verbal and performance aspects of an intelligence test, the backward readers were found to be much lower on the verbal side, and more nearly average on the performance aspects.

When all the children who had been severely backward in reading at the age of 7 and who were of average intelligence were re-tested at 9 years of age, it was found that few such children were 2 or more years backward in reading, in fact, about 1 per cent of the total population, mainly boys. These 19 children represented the incidence of severe reading disability in children of average intelligence *whatever the cause of the difficulty*. The remainder of the study was concerned with a more detailed consideration of these children.

The following points emerged in connexion with this group:

1. The majority of this group were boys (15 boys, 4 girls).

2. Only one child had all three IQs above 100 on the WISC, 9 had only their performance IQ above 90, while verbal IQ was below 90.

3. Speech defects and poor auditory discrimination were common in this group.

4. Poor visuo-motor co-ordination was shown by many of these children.

5. There was little evidence of active assistance on the part of the parents, though the parents were positive in their attitude to the work of the school. Most of the children came from large families, and the reading material seemed to be mainly that supplied by the school.

In general, the difficulties of these children were not specific to the problem of deciphering words on a printed page. It appeared that they would require assistance over a wide range of activities. The striking finding was the *diversity* of disabilities and *not* an underlying pattern common to the group. which could have provided a basis for one single remedial method for all these children. Yet the approach to the initial teaching of reading, the structure of schools, and even the home background had certain basic similarities which would not have been true in a group gathered from a wider area.

It is important, in reporting the results of a study such as the present one, to consider the implications beyond the population used here, and the extent to which generalizations would be justified.

As shown by the results of the English Picture Vocabulary Test, we were not dealing with a highly selected group of children (see pp. 42–3). If anything the group was slightly below average. Fifteen per cent of children in this study who completed 2 years at school in 1966 were still requiring some assistance with the basic skill of reading, though, as was pointed out earlier, the proportion was not necessarily the same in all schools. There is evidence from another Scottish county, where an annual survey of reading attainment is carried out on a similar age group and with a similar type of test to that used in the present study, that a similar percentage of children was 'at risk' on leaving the infant department in 1966. In that county too, children remain in the same school throughout their primary school careers from 5 to 12 years of age. In that county also, and indeed perhaps in many countries, there are problems not only of staff turn over but also of child mobility which are similar to those found in this study. It seems important, therefore, that more than an informal oral record be kept of a child's progress, so that his needs may be appreciated as soon as possible should he change school or there be staff changes within a single school.

More recent evidence from the annual surveys mentioned above would indicate that in the last few years there has been an increasing incidence of functional non-readers at the age of 7. This may be the result of delay in introducing more formal instruction, and a wider curriculum in the first 2 years, or may be merely a temporary effect of attempts to put into practice the recommendations of the official report on *Primary Education in Scotland* (Scottish Education Department, 1965) – the Scottish equivalent of the *Plowden Report* (1967). Should it be a permanent consequence of the wider curriculum, then it is important to examine its significance for teachers dealing with children who leave the infant department unable to read. As was stressed earlier, there is no particular virtue in having all children, or even most children, at a predetermined level of mechanical reading efficiency at a given age. After all, in other countries children do not start school until 6 or 7 years of age. There is evidence from comparative studies that Scottish children do score higher on mechanical tests in the 3 basic subjects at an early age, but in general others catch up at a later stage (Anderson, 1966). It may well be that a delayed start in reading and a more efficient approach at the later stage, combined with adequate grounding and appreciation of what books have to offer, is much more important than early high standards on a mechanical test. It is not intended that the results of this study be used as a plea for a return to more formal and earlier instruction in reading.

What is important is that the implications of any change be assessed and be made clear to the teachers; that in their training primary teachers, whatever age of child they may teach, be made aware of the possibility of having to deal with a child with reading difficulty; that they be able to diagnose such children, *and* that they regard it as a part of their professional duty to deal with them as far as possible. When such a case is diagnosed, with if possible some specialist guidance, the problem is in the first instance a classroom problem. Specialist help could most efficiently be used as a service to the classroom teacher. Unless his class-teacher has understanding of the needs of the backward reader, the child without adequate reading skill will find much of his school day either boring or frustrating, even if he does receive remedial instruction.

To return to the theme of the introductory chapter, the standard of teaching will determine the general level in the classroom whether it be in reading or in spelling, but within the group will still be those who require a different approach or additional help. The professional training of the teacher should prepare her to achieve the highest general level of attainment in its widest sense, *and* to deal appropriately with the individual needs within her class. Preliminary training may lay the foundation for this in making the prospective teacher aware of the differences within a group of children, and in alerting her to notice problems which she might otherwise have overlooked. In-service training should also be of value in directing her attention, when she is most highly motivated, to techniques and new approaches which may help to deal with real rather than hypothetical problems. Researches in both reading and spelling have demonstrated the importance of the 'teacher variable'. It seems important to make full use of this potential.

There was evidence that though few of the children who were very backward in reading at 7 years of age continued to be severely backward, few had made dramatic progress by the age of 9. With the shortage of teachers and overcrowded classes in the county, there were many schools with no facilities to deal with such children. In some of the larger schools where there was an infants' mistress, she concerned herself with those children who continued to have difficulty with reading. She did not feel that they ceased to be her problem when they left the infant department. This approach depended on an appreciation by the infants' mistress of the seriousness of the problem for these children, a willingness on her part to assist, and a willingness on the part of the headmaster to accept such co-operation. This temporary solution would not of course be feasible in an area where the children change school at the age of 7 or 8. As classes are reduced in size and there are adequate numbers of teachers in the primary schools, it will be important to consider the most efficient use of the available staff. To what extent is it most efficient to concentrate only on reducing class size? Is there not a point when it is better to stabilize numbers and beyond that use the teachers with appropriate training and insight to work in co-operation with the class teachers in assisting with the most severely backward children? Size is not the only criterion. Frequent short periods of instruction alone, or in small groups, linked with classroom follow-up by a teacher who has been made aware of the approach which is being tried, might well be both the most economical and efficient method of dealing with children who have difficulty, or are slow in reaching the minimum standard required for reading for enjoyment or information. The sooner the problem is tackled the less resistant it may be, and the less the unhappiness of the individual child, who may otherwise have to wait a long time for specialist treatment which might never have been necessary.

There are a number of problems in assessing the importance of the particular deficits which were found in this present study to be associated with backwardness in reading.

1. The fact that such factors were found to be associated with lack of progress in reading does not entitle one to assume that they were the *cause* of the failure in reading. Some may be, while others may be skills which could develop as a result of progress in reading. A study such as the present one does not allow conclusions as to causality to be drawn with regard to aspects

which were studied only within the population who were already backward readers. It does permit one to form hypotheses for further study. Such hypotheses are now serving as the basis for a study to assess their predictive value with regard to reading progress within a group of children beginning school.

2. Some factors, even if causal, may only be so within the type of approach to reading which is used in this county, or in Britain. There is evidence, for example, that when the approach to reading is more phonically based children with poor auditory discrimination are more vulnerable; while the more the approach emphasizes memory for whole words, the more vulnerable are children with poor visual discrimination. It is hoped to consider this aspect also in a further investigation.

3. It is important to separate those factors which are causally related to learning to read from those which are causally related to learning to read in a group situation (see p. 19). This will also be analysed further by considering the abilities and disabilities found in children who have learnt to read *before* coming in contact with the group learning situation, whether they have had assistance from an adult or not. It is important to study not only those who have difficulty in learning to read, but also those who are successful.

Even in this county, with problems of overcrowded classes, frequent staff changes, and frequent changes of school on the part of many children, only a limited number of children were found who continued to have severe problems with reading; only a small proportion of these were of average intelligence. If sufficient teachers are available , trained to teach reading, and with classes of a size to permit them to apply these skills, then the number of children with continued difficulty in reading should be minimal. Though no severely backward readers of high intelligence were found in the present study, this should not be taken to indicate that such children do not exist, though clearly they are not as common as some have suggested. With up-to-date community data on a number of aspects which have been claimed to be associated with that disability, it should now be possible to look again at such cases and consider whether, and in what ways, they differ from the most severely backward readers in a study such as this. An analysis of cases which have been diagnosed as of severe reading disability, of superior intelligence and resistant to remedial instruction, will be the final area to which the findings of this study will be applied. These are cases which a teacher will find only rarely in her teaching career, but when she does she should seek, and should be able to secure, specialist guidance; for the rest, they are a classroom problem.

Appendix

In the tables below, the scores on each test have been adjusted so that the mean score for the whole population is 100 and the standard deviation of all their scores is 15. As a result the figures in these tables have the same meaning, whichever test they refer to. A particular figure, e.g. 105 or 97, given to a group for the reading test will show that group to be as much better or worse than average as would the same figure, 105 or 97, given for the EPVT.

Reading Quotients and EPVT Scores Rescaled to Mean of 100 and Standard Deviation of 15 for Purposes of Comparison

Table A Mean Reading Quotients and EPVT Scores for Different Levels of Drawing

	Score	RQ	EPVT
High	6	106·5	106·5
	5	104·9	103·1
	4	100·2	100·5
	3	96·1	96·5
Low	2	91·3	92·3
Rescaled means		100	100

Table B Mean Reading Quotients and EPVT Scores for Different Levels of Right/Left Differentiation

Score		RQ	EPVT
High	5	105·2	104·4
	4	102·8	102·8
	3	98·5	98·4
	2	96·5	96·5
	1	91·2	91·4
Low	0	98·1	101·2
Rescaled means		100	100

Table C Mean Reading Quotients and EPVT Scores for Different Laterality Characteristics

	RQ			EPVT		
	R	L	M	R	L	M
Writing hand	100·0	99·8	*	99·9	101·2	†
Writing and throwing	100·0	99·7	100·8	99·9	102·2	99·5
Preferred foot	100·1	100·2	98·4	99·9	102·4	97·1
Preferred eye	100·2	99·8	98·9	100·4	99·2	100·2
Rescaled means	100	100	100	100	100	100

*Two cases only, 110·5.
†Two cases only, 99·6.

Table D Mean Reading Quotients and EPVT Scores for Different Absence Levels

Half-day absences	First year		Second year	
	RQ	EPVT	RQ	EPVT
0–20	101·1	99·5	102·0	101·4
21–40	100·9	100·5	100·5	100·2
41–80	100·2	100·3	98·0	98·2
81+	93·9	97·7	92·0	97·8
Not known	99·8	101·3	102·3	100·5
Rescaled means	100	100	100	100

Table E Mean Reading Quotients and EPVT Scores for Different Number of Schools Attended

	RQ	EPVT
One school only	99·8	99·5
Two or more schools within county	100·1	101·6
From outside county	102·3	102·7
No record	99·0	98·6
Rescaled means	100	100

Table F Mean Intelligence Test Scores on WISC for 230 Backward Readers Age 8 to 8 Years 5 Months

	Boys (138)		Girls (92)		Total (230)	
	Mean	SD	Mean	SD	Mean	SD
Full scale	92·8	11·0	85·3	11·9	89·8	11·9
Verbal	92·5	10·4	85·0	11·3	89·5	11·4
Performance	96·0	12·2	89·5	13·6	93·4	13·1
Verbal sub-tests						
Information	8·0	2·3	6·9	2·3	7·5	2·4
Comprehension	10·5	3·3	8·1	3·2	9·5	3·5
Arithmetic	8·2	2·3	7·8	2·4	8·1	2·4
Similarities	8·1	2·5	7·6	2·5	7·9	2·5
Vocabulary	8·2	2·4	6·4	2·4	7·5	2·6
Performance sub-tests						
Picture completion	9·5	2·7	8·8	2·8	9·2	2·8
Picture arrangement	8·6	2·9	7·5	3·1	8·2	3·0
Block design	9·0	2·8	7·8	2·7	8·5	2·8
Object assembly	11·1	2·9	9·2	3·3	10·3	3·2
Coding	8·3	2·6	8·3	3·1	8·3	2·8

Table G Intelligence and Reading of Experimental, Control and Non-Control Groups (all Children with at least One IQ 90 or More)

Intelligence on *WISC*		*Experimental*	*Mean scores*	
			control	*non-control*
Full IQ	Boys	94·4	98·6	98·5
	Girls	91·4	92·0	92·2
Verbal IQ	Boys	93·6	98·4	96·5
	Girls	88·9	90·1	90·7
Performance IQ	Boys	98·1	100·9	102·8
	Girls	97·2	97·5	96·7
Reading-Neale				
Accuracy	Boys	7·2	8·8	8·5
(in yrs and mths)	Girls	7·4	8·4	8·4
Comprehension	Boys	6·11	8·4	8·0
(in yrs and mths)	Girls	6·11	7·7	7·8
Frequencies	Boys	46	23	37
	Girls	23	19	17
Totals		*69*	*42*	*54*

Notes:

All 165 children were tested on Neale at the age of 9 – see Table 16 for results.

Experimental and control groups were the 111 children tested on the third-stage battery.

The experimental group was made up of all those with at least one IQ 90 or more and Southgate score of 21 or less.

Control and non-control together are all those with at least one IQ 90 or more and a Southgate score of 22 or more.

The experimental, control and non-control are comparable for intelligence for each sex separately.

Control and non-control are comparable for reading and better than experimental for reading – for each sex separately.

References

Anderson, I. H. (1966), 'Comparisons of the reading and spelling achievement and quality of handwriting of groups of English, Scottish and American children', *Co-operative Research Projects*, no. 1903, University of Michigan.

Balow, I. H. (1963), 'Lateral dominance characteristics and reading achievement in the first grade', *Journal of Psychology*, vol. 55, pp. 323–8.

Belmont, L., and Birch, H. G. (1965), 'Lateral dominance, lateral awareness and reading disability', *Child Development*, vol. 36, pp. 57–71.

Belmont, L., and Birch, H. (1966), 'The intellectual profile of retarded readers', *Perceptual and Motor Skills*, vol. 22, pp. 787–816.

Bender, L. (1946), *Bender Visual Motor Gestalt Test*, distributed by the National Foundation for Educational Research.

Birch, H., and Belmont, L. (1964), 'Auditory-visual integration in normal and retarded readers', *American Journal of Orthopsychiatry*, vol. 34, pp. 852–61.

Brenner, M. W., Gillman, S., Zangwill, O., and Farrell, M. (1967), 'Visuo-motor disability in schoolchildren', *British Medical Journal*, no. 4, pp. 259–62.

Brimer, M. A., and Dunn, L. M. (1963), *English Picture Vocabulary Tests*, distributed by Educational Evaluation Enterprises, Bristol.

Broadhurst, A., and Phillips, C. J. (1969), 'Reliability and validity of the Bender Gestalt Test in a sample of British schoolchildren', *British Journal of Social and Clinical Psychology*, vol. 8, pp. 253–62.

Burt, C. (1961), *The Backward Child*, 5th edn, University of London Press.

Burt, C. (1969), Foreword to *ita: An Independent Evaluation*, by F. W. Warburton and V. Southgate, Murray & Chambers.

Chall, J. (1967), *Learning to Read: The Great Debate*, McGraw-Hill.

Christine, D., and Christine, C. (1964), 'The relationship of auditory discrimination to articulatory defects and reading retardation', *Elementary School Journal*, vol. 65, pp. 97–100.

Clark, M. M. (1957), *Left-Handedness: Laterality Characteristics and their Educational Implications*, Publications of the Scottish Council for Research in Education, no. 39, University of London Press.

Clark, M. M. (1959), *Teaching Left-Handed Children*, Publications of the Scottish Council for Research in Education, no. 44, University of London Press.

Clark, M. M. (1967), 'Laterality characteristics and reading', *Reading*, vol. 1, no. 3, pp. 3–9.

Coleman, R. I., and Deutsch, C. P. (1964), 'Lateral dominance and right–left discrimination: a comparison of normal and retarded readers', *Perceptual and Motor Skills*, vol. 19, pp. 43–50.

Critchley, M. (1964), *Developmental Dyslexia*, Heinemann.

Crosby, R. M. N., and Liston, R. A. (1968), *Reading and the Dyslexic Child*, Souvenir Press.

Daniels, J. C., and Diack, H. (1958), *The Standard Reading Tests*, Chatto & Windus.

De Hirsch, K., Jansky, J. J., and Langford, W. D. (1966), *Predicting Reading Failure*, Harper & Row.

Department of Education and Science (1967), *Children and their Primary Schools (Plowden Report)*, HMSO.

Doehring, G. (1968), *Patterns of Impairment in Specific Reading Disability*, Indiana University Press.

Douglas, J. W. B., Ross, J. M., and Cooper, J. E. (1967), 'The relationship between handedness, attainment and adjustment in a national sample of schoolchildren', *Educational Research*, vol. 9, no. 3, pp. 223–32.

Durrell, D. D., and Murphy, H. A. (1953), 'The auditory discrimination factor in reading readiness and reading disability', *Education*, vol. 73, no. 9, pp. 556–60.

Enstrom, E. A. (1962), 'The extent of the use of the left hand in handwriting', *Journal of Educational Research*, vol. 55, no. 5, pp. 234–5.

Franklin, A. W. (ed.) (1958), *Word-Blindness or Specific Developmental Dyslexia*, Pitman Medical.

Gardner, K. (1968), 'State of reading', in N. Smart (ed.), *Crisis in the Classroom*, Daily Mirror Books, pp. 18–30.

Hallgren, B. (1950), 'Specific dyslexia (congenital word-blindness): a clinical and genetic study', *Acta Psychiatrica et Neurologica, Scandinavica*, supplement 65.

Hinshelwood, J. (1895), 'Word-blindness and visual memory', *Lancet*, vol. 2, pp. 1564–70.

Ingram, T. T. S., Mason, A. W., and Blackburn, I. (in press), 'A retrospective study of 82 children who suffered from difficulty in learning to read', *Development Medicine and Child Neurology*.

Kass, C. E. (1963), 'Some psychological correlates of severe reading disability (dyslexia)', in D. J. Sievers *et al.*, *Selected Studies on the Illinois Test of Psycholinguistic Abilities*, Institute for Research on Exceptional Children, University of Illinois, pp. 87–95.

Koppitz, E. M. (1958a), 'The Bender Gestalt Test and learning disturb-
ances in young children', *Journal of Clinical Psychology*, vol. 14,
pp. 292–5.

Koppitz, E. M. (1958b), 'Relationships between the Bender Gestalt Test
and the Wechsler Intelligence Test for Children', *Journal of Clinical
Psychology*, vol. 14, pp. 413–16.

Koppitz, E. M. (1964), *The Bender Gestalt Test for Young Children*, Grune
& Stratton.

Lachmann, F. M. (1960), 'Perceptual-motor development in children
retarded in reading ability', *Journal of Consulting Psychology*, vol. 24, no.
5, pp. 427–31.

Lovell, K., and Gorton, A. (1968), 'Some differences between backward and
normal readers of average intelligence', *British Journal of Educational
Psychology*, vol. 38, pt 3, pp. 240–48.

McCarthy, J. J., and Kirk, S. A. (1961), *Illinois Test of Psycholinguistic
Abilities*, experimental edn, Institute for Research on Exceptional
Children, University of Illinois.

Malmquist, E. (1958), *Factors Related to Reading Disabilities in the First
Grade of the Elementary School*, Almquist & Wiksell.

Mittler, P., and Ward, J. (1970), 'The use of the Illinois Test of Psycholinguistic Abilities on British four-year-old children: a normative and
factorial study', *British Journal of Educational Psychology*, vol. 40, pt 1,
pp. 43–54.

Money, J. (ed.) (1962), *Reading Disability: Progress and Research Needs in
Dyslexia*, Johns Hopkins Press.

Money, J., and Schiffman, G. (eds.) (1966), *The Disabled Reader*, Johns
Hopkins Press.

Monroe, M. (1932), *Children Who Cannot Read*, University of Chicago
Press.

Morris, J. M. (1966), *Standards and Progress in Reading*, National Foundation for Educational Research.

Neale, M. D. (1966), *Neale Analysis of Reading Ability*, Macmillan.

Peters, M. L. (1967), *Spelling: Caught or Taught?*, Routledge & Kegan Paul.

Phillips, C. J. (1968), 'The Illinois Test of Psycholinguistic Abilities: a
report on its use with English children and a comment on the psychological sequelae of low birth-weight', *British Journal of Disorders of
Communication*, vol. 3, pp. 143–9.

Pringle, M. L. K., Butler, N. R., and Davie, R. (1966), *11,000 Seven-Year-
Olds*, Longmans.

Reid, J. F. (1966), 'Learning to think about reading', *Educational Research*,
vol. 9, no. 1, pp. 56–62.

Reid, J. F. (1968), 'Dyslexia: a problem of communication', *Educational Research*, vol. 10, no. 2, pp. 126–33.

Robinson, H. M. (1946), *Why Pupils Fail in Reading*, University of Chicago Press.

Rutter, M. (1967), 'A children's behaviour questionnaire for completion by teachers: preliminary findings', *Journal of Child Psychology and Psychiatry*, vol. 8, pp. 1–11.

Rutter, M., Tizard, J., and Whitmore, K. (eds.) (in press), *Education, Health and Behaviour*, Longmans.

Schonell, F. J., and Schonell, F. E. (1960), *Diagnostic and Attainment Testing*, 4th edn, Oliver & Boyd.

Scottish Council for Research in Education (1965), *The Wechsler Intelligence Scale for Children*, Manual for Scottish Standardisation.

Scottish Council for Research in Education (1967), *The Scottish Standardisation of the Wechsler Intelligence Scale for Children*, Publication no. 55, University of London Press.

Scottish Education Department (1965), *Primary Education in Scotland*, HMSO, Edinburgh.

Smith, C. E., and Keogh, B. K. (1962), 'The Group Bender Gestalt as a reading readiness screening instrument', *Perceptual and Motor Skills*, vol. 15, pp. 639–45.

Smith, C. E., and Keogh, B. K. (1963), 'Developmental changes on the Bender Gestalt Test', *Perceptual and Motor Skills*, vol. 17, pp. 465–6.

Southgate, V. (1958), *Southgate Group Reading Tests*, University of London Press.

Stevenson, L. P., and Robinson, H. M. (1953), 'Eye–hand preference, reversals, and reading progress', in H. Robinson (ed.), *Clinical Studies in Reading*, University of Chicago Press, vol. 2, pp. 83–8.

Tansley, A. E. (1967), *Reading and Remedial Reading*, Routledge & Kegan Paul.

Terman, L. M., and Merrill, M. A. (1961), *Stanford-Binet Intelligence Scale*, Manual for the 3rd Revision, Form L-M, Harrap.

Thompson, B. B. (1963), 'A longitudinal study of auditory discrimination', *Journal of Educational Research*, vol. 56, no. 7, pp. 376–8.

Vernon, M. D. (1957), *Backwardness in Reading: A Study of its Nature and Origin*, Cambridge University Press.

Wechsler, D. (1949), *Wechsler Intelligence Scale for Children*, Psychological Corporation.

Wechsler, D. (1963), *Wechsler Pre-School and Primary Scale of Intelligence*, Psychological Corporation.

Wepman, J. M. (1958), *Auditory Discrimination Test*, distributed by the National Foundation for Educational Research.

Wepman, J. M. (1960), 'Auditory discrimination, speech and reading', *Elementary School Journal*, vol. 60, pp. 325–33.

Zazzo, R., and Galifret–Granjon, N. (1964), *Manuel pour l'examen psychologique de l'enfant*, pt 1, p. 31, Delachaux et Niestle.

Index

Items mentioned in the case histories are not indexed separately.